EMBROIDERY
PROJECTS
IN MINIATURE

READER'S DIGEST

EMBROIDERY
PROJECTS
IN MINIATURE

55 Step-by-Step Projects

MEG EVANS

READER'S DIGEST ASSOCIATION INC.
Pleasantville, New York / Montreal

A READER'S DIGEST BOOK
Edited and produced by David & Charles

This book is dedicated to the memory of my mother,
who enjoyed the pleasure of her embroidery into her ninety-second year.

Spring in the Garden

(Page 2) A selection of embroidered boxes including three nesting boxes, fitted circular box, hat-shaped box, pulled-work box pincushion, gold initial box, and dressing table box

(Page 6) The many different projects featured in the book include miniature pictures, tote bag, circular basket, miniature furniture and carpets in $^1/_{12}$ scale, and pulled-fabric pictures

Photography by Di Lewis

First published in the UK in 1994
Text and designs Copyright © 1994, 1997 Meg Evans
Photography and layout Copyright © 1994, 1997
David & Charles

Printed in the UK

Library of Congress Cataloging in Publication Data

Evans, Meg.
 [55 embroidery projects in miniature]
 Embroidery projects in miniature : 55 step-by-step projects / Meg Evans.
  p.   cm.
 First published in Great Britain in 1994 under title : 55 embroidery projects in miniature.
  Includes index.
  ISBN 0-89577-969-2
  1. Embroidery—Patterns.   2. Ornamental boxes.   3. Doll furniture.
 I. Title.
 TT775.E94   1997
 746.44′041—dc21   97-13239

Contents

Introduction

*T*HROUGHOUT the ages people have derived pleasure from creating beautiful things for daily use. Carpets, cushions, saddle cloths, tents, sails, and clothing were often beautifully embroidered, demonstrating the creativity of their makers. Many of today's designs are taken from historical embroidery as well as from a variety of other sources, such as architecture and old design books. When worked on traditional fabrics, such embroidery is relaxing and satisfying.

In this book I have set out to show how traditional techniques and modern materials can be used together to create a range of interesting designs for small projects that are both useful and decorative.

Plastic canvas has been available for a decade or more. Originally sold only in 7-bar mesh (7 bars to the inch), it was first used for easily made, mass-appeal items, which lacked finesse and style. It was also popular as a children's teaching aid and for elderly embroiderers with failing sight.

Some embroiderers may have reservations about the use of plastic canvas, but, in my view, since it is completely covered by the embroidery and therefore not seen, these are misplaced. Plastic canvas has many advantages: It is easy to handle and will not go out of shape; it is rigid and therefore ideal for constructed items such as boxes; and it is washable. However, it does lack the suppleness of cotton canvas, and the finest gauge available (14-bar mesh) is not very strong. Plastic canvas will never replace cotton canvas, but in appropriate situations it is unbeatable. (See Chapter 11 for more details on plastic canvas.)

The projects in this book use both traditional materials and plastic canvas. Some, such as the canvas work and pulled-work pincushions and needlecases, are completely traditional. Others, like the bags and baskets in Chapter 1, are on plastic canvas only. In others I have used combinations of embroidery on natural fabrics, embroidery on plastic canvas, and plastic canvas covered by fabric to achieve the desired effect.

The range of possibilities is enormous – and I have written this book to encourage others to begin experimenting with the old and the new. I hope you find the process as enjoyable as I have! Please note that it is advisable to read Chapter 11, which explains the techniques and basic methods used throughout the book, before starting any of the projects.

– 1 –
Bags and Baskets

*T*HESE small bags and baskets are quick to make, and they can be used in a great variety of ways. You can fill them with flowers, Easter eggs, or special small gifts – or delight the heart of any small girl with a hat-shaped box for her special treasures.

The baskets would make attractive table decorations for a special occasion. For a wedding, they could be stitched in colors that complement the bride's color scheme and filled with flowers to match the bride's bouquet. The bridegroom's gifts to the bridesmaids, if small enough, could be presented in the hatboxes, with the ribbon made from the same material as their dresses.

For a new baby, the dainty cradle would make a delightful gift stitched in pink or blue with matching embroidered bed linen.

The bag and basket designs detailed here are just a few suggestions – let your imagination get to work, and make them in any size or color you wish.

Large and small circular baskets, cradle, hatboxes, and tote bag

Tote Bag

A miniature tote, like a doll's shopping bag, seems to have universal appeal. It is the perfect size for presenting a small but special gift, such as jewelry or a lace handkerchief.

    This little bag is worked using 10-bar plastic canvas. If a larger bag is preferred, using 7-bar canvas instead of 10-bar would more than double the capacity. The border could be made wider by increasing the number of rows of tent stitch, or by adding one in double cross stitch. The inner cream area, or the size of the leaves, could be enlarged. Remember that the central flower is the focal point of the design, and you should aim to keep a balance between the two sections.

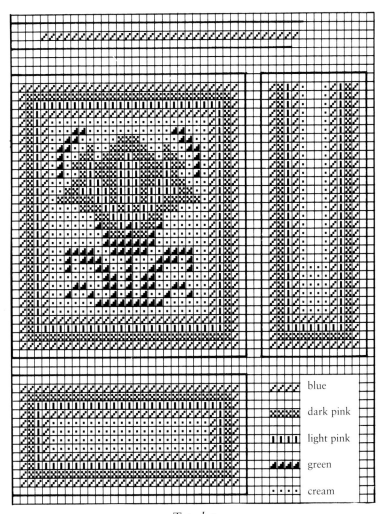

Tote bag

⁄⁄⁄⁄	blue
✗✗✗✗	dark pink
⊥⊥⊥⊥⊥	light pink
◢◢◢◢	green
· · · ·	cream

MATERIALS

10 x 5in (250 x 125mm) plastic canvas, 10 bars
    per inch (25mm)
Anchor Pearl cotton No. 5
    two skeins: 161 blue
    one skein each of: 73 light pink; 75 dark pink;
    216 green
Paterna Stranded Yarn
    two skeins: 263 cream

From the plastic canvas, cut two sides 33 x 31 bars, two gussets 33 x 14 bars, one base 31 x 14 bars, and two handles 42 x 3 bars.

Use pearl cotton singly for the cross stitch, doubled for the tent stitch and overcasting. Use a single strand of cream yarn for the cross stitch.

Work the central patterned area in cross stitch. Tent stitch is used elsewhere.

HANDLES

Leaving the first and last four bars of canvas uncovered, work a single line of tent stitch down the center in light pink. Overcast the edges beside the stitching in blue. Baste the handles behind the upper edge of each side piece, underlapping by four bars and making sure that the handles are evenly spaced.

FIG. 1 Stitch diagram for handles

SIDES AND BASE

For the sides, work the embroidery following the chart, taking the stitches through the handles at the same time. Start with the top row of blue pearl cotton to anchor the handles in place. Embroider the base following the chart.

GUSSETS

Embroider the gussets, leaving the two center bars uncovered as shown. Carefully cut between the two uncovered bars, leaving the last bar uncut. Trim off the spikes. Fold gusset in half lengthwise, with right sides inside and edges matched up, and, starting at the lower end, overcast to join. For extra strength, work to the top of the gusset and down again.

TO MAKE THE BAG

Place the lower edge of one side against the base, with edges matching and wrong sides facing. Overcast together using blue pearl. Join the gussets and the other side in the same way. Join the corners and overcast the top edge, taking the stitching through the handles as you work.

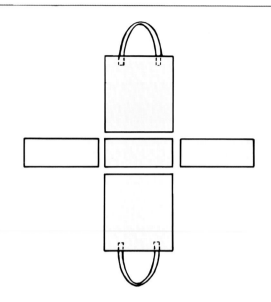

FIG. 2 *Assembling the tote bag*

Circular Basket

This decorative basket could be used for presents or candy, or filled with flowers. For Easter, it could be stitched in yellow and green and decorated with fresh flowers or Easter eggs.

The basket is lined with a second piece of plastic canvas, which gives extra stability and provides a neat finish. The size of the basket can be varied by using any of the preformed plastic-canvas circles.

LARGE BASKET

MATERIALS

14 x 6in (355 x 150mm) plastic canvas, 10 bars
   per inch (25 mm)
4¼in (106mm) diameter plastic-canvas circle
Paterna Stranded Yarn
   four skeins: 263 cream
Anchor Pearl Cotton No. 5
   one skein each of: 161 blue; 76 dark pink;
   73 light pink; 216 green

From the plastic canvas, cut one side 135 x 18 bars, one lining 130 x 17 bars, one backing strip 8 x 18 bars, one backing strip 8 x 17 bars, and one handle 96 x 8 bars.

Use the pearl cotton singly for the cross and edge stitch, doubled for the tent stitch and overcasting. Use a single strand of yarn for the cross stitch, three strands for the satin stitch.

Large and small circular baskets

HANDLE

Leaving four bars of the plastic canvas uncovered at each end, work cross stitch as shown in the chart. Edge stitch beside the embroidery in blue.

SIDE

Baste the (8 x 18) backing strip to the right short edge of the side piece so that it underlaps by four bars. Following the chart, embroider the side piece, leaving four bars uncovered at each end. Lap the left-hand edge over the backing strip to join it into a ring and complete the embroidery through both layers.

FIG. 3 Backing strip to side

FIG. 4 Joining into a ring

BASE

Work rounds of satin stitch, covering the central intersection with a cross stitch.

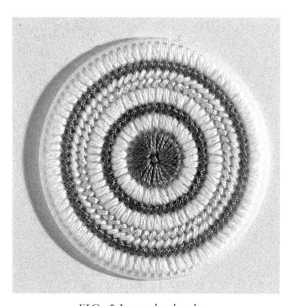

FIG. 5 Large basket base

LINING

Mark the center of the lining piece with a knot. With the wrong side of the handle facing the lining, baste the handle in place, underlapping by four bars, four bars to the left of the marked center. Baste the 8 x 17 backing strip to the right short edge, underlapping it by four bars. Leaving four bars uncovered at the left short edge, work sloping lines of small diagonal stitch to within about 1½in (40mm) of the right edge.

Baste the left-hand edge over the backing strip, right side facing in, to form a ring. Baste the free end of the handle beside the backing strip, underlapping it by the four uncovered bars. Complete the embroidery through both layers. Overcast around the lower edge.

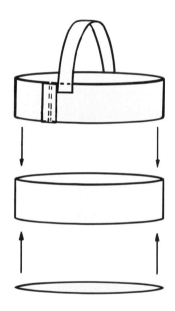

FIGS. 6 and 7 Basket into ring and Stitching up basket

TO FINISH THE BASKET

Place the side over the base and overcast, in blue, all around to join. As the base piece has larger holes than the side, stitch twice into the same hole of the base where necessary. Place the lining inside and edge stitch all around the upper edge to join the two layers, taking the stitches through the handle at the same time.

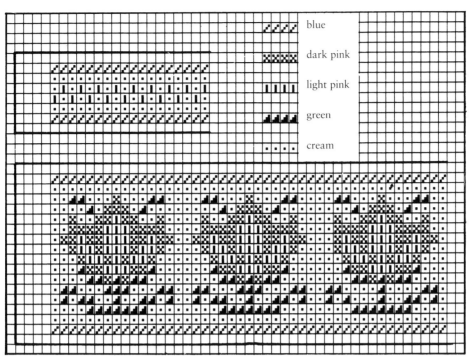

(above) Large basket   (below) Small basket

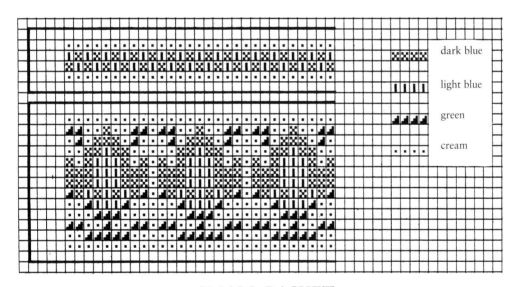

SMALL BASKET

MATERIALS

10 x 4½in (250 x 113mm) plastic canvas, 10 bars
    per inch (25mm)
3in (75mm) diameter plastic-canvas circle
Paterna Stranded Yarn
    three skeins: 263 cream
Anchor Pearl Cotton No. 5
    one skein each of: 161 blue; 975 light blue;
    216 green

From one plastic canvas, cut one side 90 x 13 bars, one lining 86 x 12 bars, one backing strip 8 x 13 bars and one 8 x 12 bars, and one handle 64 x 6 bars.

Proceed as for the large basket, following the chart above.

The Hat Box

This little hat-shaped box is made in two parts. The inner crown is attached to a circle for the base, and the outer crown fits on top.

Detailed instructions and materials are given for making the medium-sized hat; for smaller and larger sizes, the materials are given.

Plastic-canvas circles are available in standard sizes up to 12in (300mm) diameter, but any size could be cut.

MEDIUM HAT

MATERIALS

10 x 3in (250 x 75mm) plastic canvas, 7 bars per inch (25mm)

10 x 1in (250 x 25mm) plastic canvas, 10 bars per inch (25mm)

4¼in (106mm) and 3in (75mm) diameter plastic-canvas circles

Paterna Stranded Yarn
  three skeins: 263 cream

Anchor Pearl Cotton No. 5
  one skein: 161 blue
  small quantities of: 216 green; 76 dark pink; 74 light pink

From the 7-bar plastic canvas, cut one side 65 x 8 bars and one inner crown 60 x 7 bars. From the 10-bar plastic canvas, cut one band 98 x 8 bars.

Use three strands of yarn throughout. Use pearl cotton singly for the cross stitch, doubled for the overcasting.

SIDES

Leaving four bars of canvas uncovered at each short edge of the side piece (65 x 8), work rows of brick stitch over two bars in cream yarn. Overlap the short edges, matching up the bars, and complete the embroidery through both layers, forming a ring. Slip the needle under the last bar and overcast the edge to neaten. Repeat for the inner crown. Overcast along one edge on each piece.

CIRCLES

Work in rounds of satin and tent stitch as shown in Fig. 5, leaving the sixth bar from the edge uncovered on the larger circle. The inner crown will be stitched along this line. Work a cross stitch over the center intersection.

BAND

Leaving the first and last four bars uncovered, work rows of cross stitch following the chart on page 15 for the large basket handle. Overlap the ends and complete the embroidery through both layers. Overcast both edges in blue.

TO MAKE THE HAT BOX

Place the smaller circle in position over the uncovered edge of the side section, and overcast all around to join. Place the inner crown over the larger circle, uncovered bars matched up, and overcast to join them. Slip the band into place.

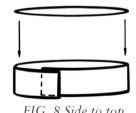

FIG. 8 Side to top

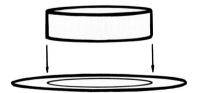

FIG. 9 Crown to base

Large, medium, and small hat boxes and cradle

LARGE HAT

MATERIALS

12 x 3in (300 x 75mm) plastic canvas, 7 bars
   per inch (25mm)
5¾in (146mm) diameter plastic-canvas circle
4¼in (106mm) diameter plastic-canvas circle
   with one bar cut from the outer edge
Paterna Stranded Yarn
   five skeins: 263 cream
18in (500mm) of 1in (23mm) wide pink ribbon
18in (500mm) of 1in (23mm) wide patterned
   ribbon

From the plastic canvas, cut one side 82 x 8
bars and one inner crown 76 x 7 bars.

Use three strands of yarn throughout, and
leave the eighth bar from the edge uncovered.

Assemble the hat in the same way as the medium hat, but omit the embroidered band. Cut
the ribbon to fit around the crown of the hat,
adding ½in (13mm) at each end for the seam.
Join each piece of ribbon into a circle and slip
over the crown. Offset the ribbon so that the
pink ribbon shows behind the patterned ribbon.

SMALL HAT

MATERIALS

6 x 2in (150 x 50mm) plastic canvas, 7 bars per
   inch (25mm)
7 x 1in (175 x 25mm) plastic canvas, 10 bars
   per inch (25mm)
Two 3in (75mm) diameter plastic-canvas circles
   (one with four bars cut from the outer edge)
Paterna Stranded Yarn
   three skeins: 263 cream
Anchor Pearl Cotton
   small quantities of: 216 green; 76 dark pink;
   74 light pink

From the 7-bar plastic canvas, cut one side 41
x 7 bars and one inner crown 34 x 6 bars. From
the 10-bar plastic canvas, cut one band 64 x 8
bars.

Use three strands of yarn throughout, and
leave the fifth bar from the edge uncovered. Use
pearl cotton singly for the cross stitch, doubled
for the overcasting.

Make the small hat in the same way as the
medium hat.

The Cradle

*This charming cradle would be perfect for a tiny doll or as a gift for
a new baby. If the cradle is being made for a special occasion, rather
than as a toy, the bedding could be embroidered in more detail. The
quilt could feature an initial or a nursery motif in cross stitch, and the
pillow could have a border of tiny flowers to make it extra pretty.*

*Square-mesh circles are used for the cradle ends, since they can be
cut to the required shape. The ends are doubled to give a neat finish
on both sides.*

MATERIALS

4in (100mm) square of plastic canvas, 7 bars per
   inch (25mm)
Four 3in (75mm) diameter square-mesh plastic-
   canvas circles
Paterna Stranded Yarn
   three skeins: 263 cream

Anchor Pearl Cotton No. 5
   one skein: 76 pink or 161 blue
Two 5 x 4in (125 x 100mm) pieces of "Linda"
   or other soft counted-thread fabric, 27 threads
   per inch (25mm)
8 x 4in (200 x 100mm) cotton fabric
12in (300mm) square of batting

From the plastic canvas, cut two sides 22 x 9 bars and one base 22 x 15 bars. From the light-weight cotton, cut one mattress piece 4 x 3in (100 x 75mm) and one pillow piece 5 x 4in (125 x 100mm).

Use the pearl cotton doubled and two strands of yarn.

SIDES AND BASE

For the sides, work a line of alternating long and short cross stitch along the top edge of the canvas in pink or blue pearl. Work three rows of long cross stitch in cream. Work one row in pink or blue. Fill in with a line of alternating long and short cross stitch in cream. Cover the base with lines of long cross stitch in cream.

FOOTBOARD

Very carefully cut away the sides of two circles to give straight edges as shown. Cut off the upper five bars to give a straight edge. The remaining section should be twelve bars deep.

For the outer section, work a line of alternating long and short cross stitch in pink or blue pearl along the upper straight edge of one piece. Fill in with cream yarn. For the inner section, on the other piece, leaving two bars uncovered at each side edge, work a line of alternating long and short cross stitch in pink or blue along the upper edge.

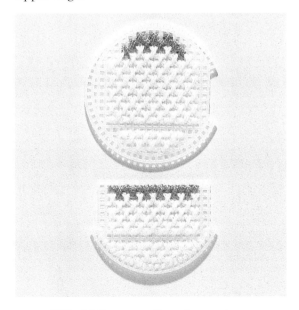

FIG. 10 Inner cradle ends, partly cut

Complete the embroidery in cream, leaving the fourth bar up from the base uncovered. The cradle base will be joined along this bar.

HEADBOARD

For the outer section, work a line of three long cross stitches along the first straight bar at the top, followed by a line of four stitches, then a single stitch at each side. Fill in the curved top with small cross and straight stitches, as necessary, to produce a good cover. Complete the embroidery in cream.

For the inner section, embroider as above, leaving two bars uncovered at each straight edge as for the footboard, and the fourth bar from the lower edge uncovered as before.

TO FINISH THE CRADLE

Overcast the two sides to the base. Overcast a short edge of each side to the inner foot section, taking the stitches over the vertical bar next to the straight edge. Overcast the base to the uncovered horizontal bar. Repeat for the headboard. Place the outer end sections in position, with the wrong sides facing, and edge stitch all around.

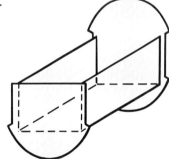

FIG. 11 Construction of cradle

CRADLE BEDDING

Make the mattress and pillow as instructed in Chapter 11, pages 118–19.

For the quilt, work a 2½ x 1⅞in (65 x 50mm) rectangle of four-sided edge stitch in the center of the two pieces of fabric. Inside this rectangle, work two rows of stem stitch in pink or blue pearl. Cut two pieces of batting slightly smaller than the quilt fabric. Overcast the two fabric sections together, using the same thread as that used for the embroidery and sandwich the batting in between.

– 2 –
Pincushions and Needlecases

Pincushions and needlecases offer some of the most rewarding practical projects for the embroiderer. Because they are small and quickly made, they are ideal projects for learning a new technique. Although made in a few hours, they nevertheless give lasting pleasure, not only to the maker but also to the user. When my mother died at the age of ninety-one, I found in her workbox the needlecase my brother had made for her at school more than sixty years before.

I once bought a needlecase at a craft sale. It was apparently made by a child, and was not really very neat or beautiful. I felt it would be adequate until I had time to make a replacement. Now, though I have several of my own design, I will not part with the original, and it is still in constant use – a reminder of the effort and concentration expended by its unknown maker.

Pincushions and needlecases

Cotton Canvas Pincushion and Needlecase

Embroidery on cotton canvas is one of the oldest and most widely used forms of needlework. The fabric is almost completely covered on both sides, so any items made by this method will be extremely durable and able to withstand constant piercing by pins and needles for a long time.

When working on cotton canvas, half cross stitch is recommended for the main embroidery to avoid distortion. It is usual to start in the center of the chart and work out. However, to make counting easier, you may prefer to work the border first. In this case, start with the double cross stitch, and make sure this is correctly placed before continuing. The materials are enough for the pincushion and needlecase.

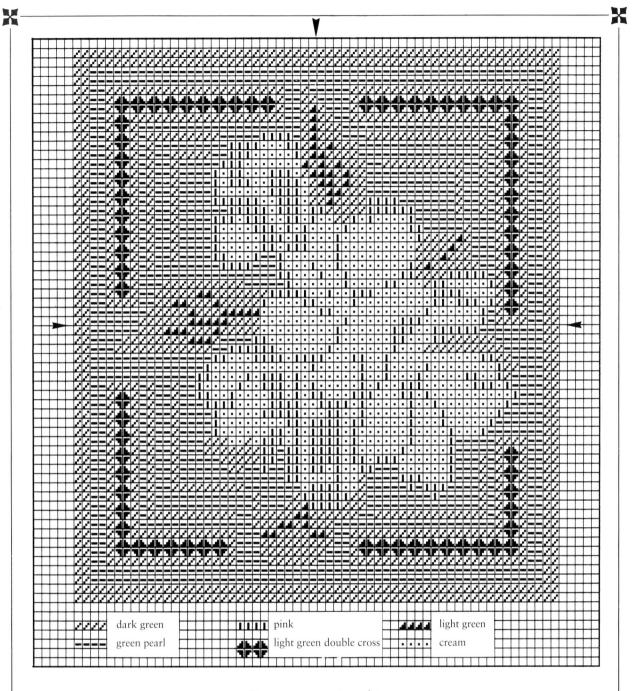

	dark green			pink
	green pearl			light green double cross		light green
						cream

Cotton canvas pincushion

MATERIALS

10 x 12in (250 x 300mm) cotton canvas,
   14 threads per inch (25mm)
7 x 10in (175 x 250mm) lining fabric
13 x 5in (330 x 130mm) interfacing
6 x 3½in (150 x 90mm) flannel or Aida
Batting
Paterna Stranded Yarn
   five skeins: 601 dark green

two skeins: 263 cream
one skein each of: 604 light green; 904 pink
Anchor Stranded Floss
   one skein: 891 yellow
Anchor Pearl Cotton No. 5
   two skeins: 214 light green
Dark green sewing thread
Embroidery frame

From the cotton canvas, cut a 6in (150mm) square for the pincushion and one piece 8 x 5½in (200 x 140mm) for the needlecase. From the lining fabric, cut a 5¼in square and one piece 8 x 5½in (200 x 140mm).

Separate the yarn and use two strands. Use the pearl cotton singly, and all six strands of the stranded floss.

PINCUSHION

Mount the canvas in the frame. Work the embroidery in half cross stitch following the chart, starting at the center and working out. Add the French knots in yellow stranded floss, referring to the photograph for position.

Remove the canvas from the frame and press from the wrong side. Trim the surplus canvas at the edge to ½in (13mm). Trim the corners leaving at least three threads of canvas for turning. Work edge stitch for cotton canvas, all around.

BACKING THE PINCUSHION

Cut a square of interfacing a little smaller than the canvas to fit just inside the edge stitch. Place the lining right side down with the interfacing centrally over it. Fold the seam allowances over the interfacing and press. Trim the corners and baste in place. Place over the embroidery, wrong sides facing, and baste.

Using the dark green sewing thread, slipstitch the lining in place, leaving a small opening for stuffing at the center of one side. The stitches should lie between the embroidery and the edge stitch, and should be closely spaced. They will scarcely show on the right side. Stuff the pincushion and complete the slipstitching.

NEEDLECASE

Work as for the pincushion, but before working the edge stitch around the perimeter, shape the spine as follows: fold the canvas along the uncovered threads on one side of the spine, so that the holes line up. Work edge stitch to cover. Repeat for the second side. Prepare and stitch the lining in place as for the pincushion, omitting the stuffing.

Finish the edges of the flannel "page" by working a line of herringbone stitch all around the outer edge, about ½in (13mm) from the edge. Turn the fabric over and work a second line on the reverse, over the first one. This gives a neat decorative edge on both sides. Start and finish the stitching on the reverse side at the center fold line, where it will show least. Fray the fabric out to the stitching.

Finger-press the central fold of the flannel "page," place inside the cover, and stitch in place along the center of the spine. Needles may be stored in the page and the cover linings.

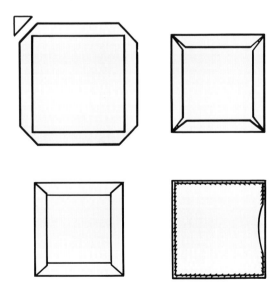

FIG. 12 Making a pincushion

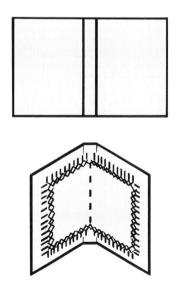

FIG. 13 Making a needlecase

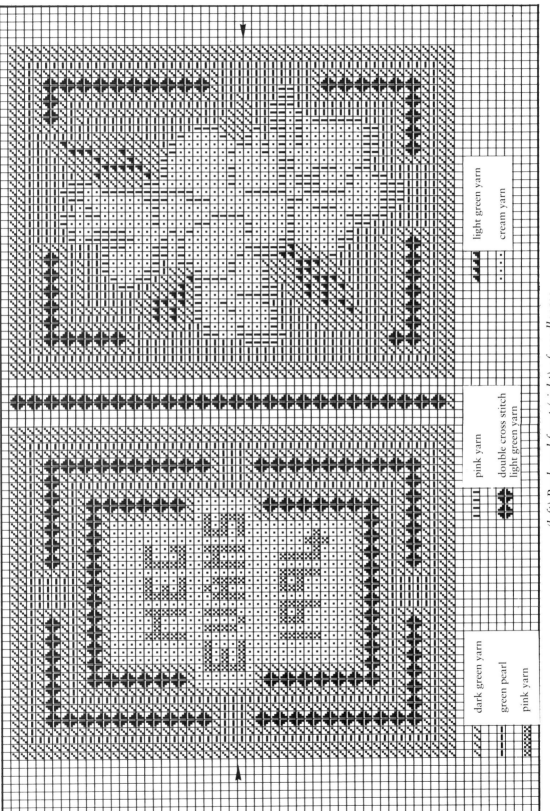

light green yarn

cream yarn

pink yarn

double cross stitch
light green yarn

dark green yarn

green pearl

pink yarn

(left) Back and front (right) of needlecase

Pulled-work Pincushion and Needlecase

This traditional form of embroidery is usually worked in cream threads on cream fabric. The thickness of the thread used in the embroidery should be similar to that of the threads in the fabric. The stitches are worked at a tight tension, pulling the fabric into holes. The tighter the tension, the larger the holes become. The pulled-work areas may be combined with surface stitching, which is often very chunky, giving added beauty and texture to the work.

Many exquisite examples on very fine fabric have survived from the past. The examples given here are on a fairly coarse linen which has 18 threads to the inch (25mm). The stitches are very simple, so both the pincushion and the needlecase can be quickly made. The pincushion has decorative lines of stitching with spaces between. In the needlecase the bands of stitching are closer, producing a slightly different effect.

Various furnishing and dress fabrics are suitable for pulled work. The weave must be even in both directions and easy enough to see. If you are using a light-colored fabric, check that it is washable.

Three surface embroidery stitches are used here: stem, satin, and raised chain band. Four-sided stitch is the only pulled-work stitch in the embroidery. A slightly different version of this is used for the edging. There are many other stitches that could be used to produce a variety of interesting textures once the pulled work is mastered.

Specialty books recommend working in a frame, as this makes counting easier and the tension more even. However, for the small pieces shown here, an embroidery frame is not absolutely necessary. The materials given are enough to make both the pincushion and needlecase.

MATERIALS

13 x 12in (330 x 305mm) evenweave linen, 18 threads per inch (25mm)
10in (250mm) square of lightweight cotton or cotton blend
9 x 8in (230 x 200mm) heavyweight interfacing
Batting
Anchor Pearl Cotton No. 5
three skeins: 926 cream
Anchor Stranded Floss
one skein: 926 cream
Embroidery frame (optional)

For the pincushion, cut two 6in (150mm) squares of evenweave linen, one piece 10 x 5in (250 x 125mm) of lightweight cotton, and one piece 8 x 5in (200 x 125mm) of interfacing. For the needlecase, cut one piece 9 x 7in (225 x 175mm) of evenweave linen, one piece 7⅝ x 4½in (190 x 115mm) of lightweight cotton, and one piece 7 x 3⅞in (175 x 97mm) of interfacing.

Use pearl cotton singly and three strands of stranded floss.

Pulled-work pincushion and needlecase, and circular pincushion box with pin compartment

PINCUSHION

Following the diagram and starting at the center, work the pincushion embroidery. Remove from the frame, if using, and work four-sided edge stitch all around. The first line of thread to be pulled out should be four threads outside the embroidery.

To avoid mistakes in counting, pull out the threads and work the stitches on the first side only. Then sew each side in turn. Work four-sided edge stitch around the edge of the second piece, for the back, making it the same size as the first.

COMPLETING THE PINCUSHION

Place the two pieces together, right sides facing out. Overcast to join around three sides, taking the stitches over the edge in each dip in the four-sided stitch.

Make a cushion pad a little larger than the embroidery (see Chapter 11, page 118). Slip the pad into the pincushion, and complete the slip stitching to close the opening.

NEEDLECASE

The needlecase is made in two pieces, which are stitched together down one long edge on completion of the embroidery.

Embroider two pieces following the diagram. Work four-sided edge stitch all around both pieces. For this, the first thread to be removed should be four threads outside the embroidery.

Place the two sections together, wrong sides facing in, and overcast down one long edge to join, taking the stitches through each dip in the edge stitch. Insert the lining and "page" as shown in the canvas needlecase (Fig. 13, page 24).

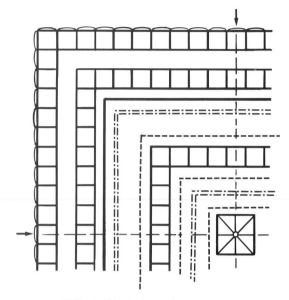

FIG. 14 Pulled-work pincushion

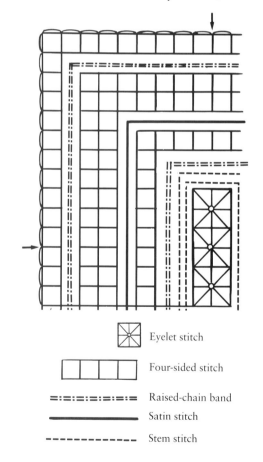

⊠	Eyelet stitch
⬜⬜⬜⬜	Four-sided stitch
=·=·=·=·=·	Raised-chain band
——	Satin stitch
- - - - - -	Stem stitch

FIG. 15 Pulled-work needlecase

Pulled-work Box Pincushion / Needleholder

This box pincushion is worked in natural fabrics but has a plastic-canvas lining instead of the usual cardboard to simplify the construction. The pulled-work top is attached to the canvas-work side, which is lined with plastic canvas to make a deep lid. The lid cleverly lifts off the base to reveal a pin box and needleholder. The needleholder fits inside the lid, which has a small pearl button knob.

In complete contrast to the traditional method of the previous pulled-work example, this pincushion top is embroidered with free-hand pulled work, stitched on a loosely woven lightweight fabric. No counting of threads is necessary; the stitches are worked freely, combining the chosen colors by eye for a pleasing effect.

The example contains seven different colors of stranded floss, though fewer colors could be used if preferred.

MATERIALS

12 x 3in (300 x 75mm) cotton canvas, 12 threads per inch (25mm)

10 x 4in (250 x 100mm) plastic canvas, 7 bars per inch (25mm)

Three 3in (75mm) diameter plastic-canvas circles

6in (150mm) square of voile

8 x 4in (200 x 100mm) lightweight wool fabric

12 x 8in (300 x 200mm) cotton or cotton blend lining fabric

Two pieces 8⅞ x 3in (220 x 75mm) lining fabric, cut on the bias

6 x 3in (150 x 75mm) heavyweight interfacing

7in (180mm) square of batting

Anchor Stranded Floss
three skeins: 879 dark green
one skein each of: 876 light green; 68 dark pink; 271 light pink; 118 dark iris; 95 light iris; 305 yellow

⅜in (10mm) diameter chunky pearl button

12 x 3in (300 x 75mm) of 1mm cardboard

Clear glue

Vanishing pencil

Embroidery frame

4in (100mm) embroidery hoop

From the plastic canvas, cut one pincushion side 63 x 10 bars, one pincushion inner lid 56 x 4 bars, and one pin box side 56 x 6 bars.

Use six strands of stranded floss on the cotton canvas and twelve strands on the plastic canvas.

CANVAS SIDE STRIP

Mount the cotton canvas onto the frame. Leaving the first 1in (25mm) uncovered, work 9Hin (238mm) in lines of long cross stitch as listed below. The first and last lines will need to be filled in with small stitches along the edge. Follow the sequence:

1) dark green; 2) dark pink; 3) medium green; 4) light pink; 5) dark lilac; 6) dark green; 7) light lilac; 8) dark pink; 9) light green; 10) light pink; 11) dark lilac; 12) medium green; 13) light lilac; 14) dark pink; 15) dark green.

Remove the canvas from the frame and press from the wrong side. Fold with right sides facing, and back stitch along the line of the embroidery to join into a ring. Check on the right side that the canvas does not show on the seam line. Press the seam, and turn to the right side. This sleeve will fit over the plastic canvas lining to form the lid side.

Work edge stitch in dark green along both edges, using the technique for cotton canvas (see Chapter 12, page 123).

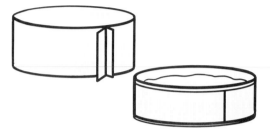

FIG. 16 Canvas pincushion side

EMBROIDERED PINCUSHION LID

Mark the area to be embroidered on the light-weight fabric with a disappearing pencil. The area should be just a little larger than the plastic-canvas circle. Place the fabric in the hoop frame, making sure that it is drum-tight. Work flower shapes in straight stitch, filling in with French knots to cover the marked area. Remove from the frame.

PREPARING THE LINING

Cut three circles of the cotton or cotton blend lining fabric, and two of the wool fabric, to the size of the plastic-canvas circles plus ½in (13mm) extra all around for seam allowances.

Cut a circle of cardboard slightly smaller than the plastic-canvas circles. The edge should be between the two outer bars, allowing room for the needle to pass through when embroidering the edge. Cover with lining fabric, one for the inside base of the pin box, the other for the underside of the pincushion section.

Trim one bar off the outer edge of a second plastic-canvas circle and cut two circles of cardboard slightly smaller. Cover with lining fabric, one for the inside base of the pin box, the other for the underside of the pincushion section.

Cut two circles of interfacing the same size as the covered cardboard. Cover each with wool fabric and slip stitch to each side of the trimmed plastic-canvas circle for the needleholder. Stitch

the pearl button to the center of one side. Needles may be stored on both sides.

PREPARING THE PINCUSHION

Cut a circle of lining fabric the size of the plastic-canvas circle plus ½in (13mm) seam allowance all around. Cut a circle of cardboard slightly smaller than the plastic-canvas circle. Cut four circles of batting, one the size of the plastic-canvas circle and the other three in decreasing size.

Run a line of small running stitches around the outer edge of one circle of lining fabric ⅜in (10mm) in from the edge. Fasten on securely, but do not fasten off.

FIG. 17 Padding the pincushion

Place the lining circle right side down and center the largest circle of batting over it. Add the other three batting circles in order of decreasing size. Place the cardboard circle over this. Pull up the stitching so that the cardboard and batting are enclosed. Check that there is enough batting to make a good dome, adding more if necessary. This padded circle should be a loose fit inside the cotton-canvas side, so that when it is covered with the embroidery, it fits snugly. Try the circle in position, as the size of the cardboard could be adjusted if necessary at this stage. If all is well, pull up the stitching really tightly and fasten off securely.

Using a plastic-canvas circle as a guide, trim the pulled-work embroidery into a circle, allowing at least 1in (25mm) extra all around. Sew a line of running stitches around the edge without fastening off, as before. Place this right side down with the prepared pad, also right side down, over it. Pull up the stitching tightly as for the lining, and fasten off securely.

TO MAKE THE PINCUSHION

For the main lining, overlap the plastic canvas (63 x 10) for the pincushion side by four bars and stitch securely in place to form a ring. Try this inside the cotton-canvas sleeve, to make sure the size is correct, and adjust the overlap if necessary.

Join one of the bias strips of lining fabric into a ring, press the seam, and place inside the plastic canvas, adjusting the length if necessary. Turn the edges to the outside, and baste in position. Slip this inside the cotton-canvas sleeve. The lower edge of the plastic canvas should be level with the edge of the cotton-canvas, the upper edge slightly lower. Slip stitch all around the lower edge using three strands of dark green. Remove the basting.

PINCUSHION LID INNER SIDE

Overlap the short edges of the plastic canvas (56 x 4) by four bars and stitch securely together to form a ring. Overcast the top edge. Any yarn will do; it will not be visible, but is needed to help the glue adhere. Place the ring against the wrong side of the smaller fabric-covered circle, and overcast to join, making a shallow box shape.

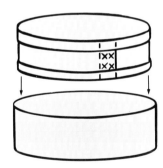

FIG. 18 Lining the pincushion

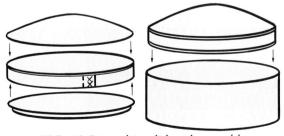

FIG. 19 Pincushion lid and assembly

Spread glue around the top edge of the box and around the edge of the base of the pincushion. Place the pincushion over the box section, and let it set.

Spread glue inside the embroidered pincushion side and place the box inside with the edges level. Hold in place until glue is set.

THE PIN BOX

Turn under about ¼in (5mm) on one long edge of the bias strip for covering the pin box side. Place the fold close to the lower edge of the plastic canvas (56 x 6) and slip stitch in place, trimming the short ends to ⅜in (10mm). Turn the ends over the plastic canvas. Place the two short edges together, wrong sides facing, and overcast securely to join into a ring. The seam may poke out slightly, but this method avoids bulk.

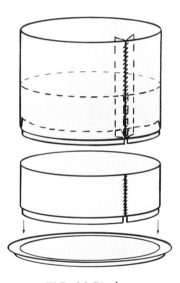

FIG. 20 Pin box

Place the ring over a plastic-canvas circle and overcast to join to the bar next to the edge of the circle. Fold the free edge of the fabric to the inside, and smooth the spare fabric over the base.

Edge stitch all around the outer bar of the base with twelve strands of green stranded floss using the plastic-canvas technique (see Chapter 12, pages 122–23).

Slip the smaller lined cardboard circle inside the box. When closing the pin box, place the needle holder on the pin box, button side down, then place the embroidered pincushion lid on top.

Fabric and Plastic-Canvas Pincushion and Needlecase

For this matching pincushion and needleholder set, the flower motif has been covered with embroidery worked in matching stranded floss. The same fabric, without embroidery, is used for lining the needlecase – cut to display the flower motif in the center of the cover. The sides of the pincushion and the frame of the needlecase are worked on plastic canvas, in colors to match the embroidery.

MATERIALS

10 x 6in (250 x 150mm) plastic canvas, 10 bars
 per inch (25mm)
15 x 4in (380 x 100mm) patterned fabric
15 x 4in (380 x 100mm) interfacing
12in (300mm) square of batting
Anchor Stranded Floss
 two skeins in each of your chosen colors

Colors are not given since they will depend on the fabric. The quantities specified are enough for both pincushion and needlecase.

From the plastic canvas, for the pincushion, cut four sides 28 x 9 bars and two pieces for the top and base 28 bars square. For the needlecase, cut two sides 30 x 24 bars and one spine 30 x 3 bars.

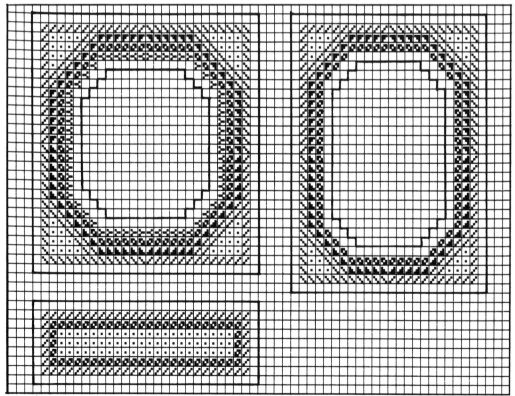

(left) Pincushion and (right) needlecase

Fabric and plastic-canvas pincushion and needlecase, and
hat-shaped thimble holder and needlecase

Use twelve strands of floss for the tent stitch and six for the edge stitch on plastic canvas. Use three strands on the fabric.

Embroider the flowers on the fabric by outlining the shapes in stem stitch and then filling in with straight stitch, working French knots in the center of the flowers.

Embroider the plastic canvas. Put in extra stitches on the slanting lines at each corner where the canvas will be cut. This avoids filling in these gaps when working the overcasting.

Very carefully cut out the inner uncovered areas, taking care to leave one bar all around beside the embroidery. Overcast the inner edges.

PREPARING THE FABRIC

Interfacing: Cut one square just slightly smaller than the plastic canvas for the pincushion top. Cut two pieces the size of a single needlecase cover. Cut one piece the size of the inside of the needlecase, across the spine and both covers.

Fabric: Cut the embroidered panels a fraction smaller than the outer edge of the plastic canvas. Press on the wrong side.

Batting: Cut three pieces for the pincushion: one the size of the interfacing, one slightly smaller, and the third smaller still. Cut six pieces for the needlecase: two the size of the opening, two slightly smaller, and two even smaller.

TO FINISH

Place the fabric for the pincushion right side down with the pieces of batting on top in order of size, largest first, followed by the square of interfacing. Use running stitches to join the three layers together, just inside the edge. Position these stitches so that they will not show when the embroidered frame is placed over them. Test behind the frame to make sure there is enough batting for the fabric to make a nice dome shape.

More may be inserted if wished. Glue or stitch in position on the back of the frame section. Prepare the needlecase covers in the same way.

Stitch the sides of the pincushion to the top, and join the corners to form a box shape. Attach the prepared base stuffing with batting before completing the stitching.

Join the covers of the needlecase to the spine and edge stitch all around. Cut and insert the lining and page, as in the cotton-canvas version on page 24.

Hat-shaped Thimble Holder and Needlecase

Imported hat-shaped needlecases were popular when I was a child. This modern version is stronger and more durable than they were, and, since it takes very little time to make, it would be ideal as a small gift or bazaar item.

MATERIALS

4 x 3in (100 x 75mm) plastic canvas, 10 bars per inch (25mm)

Three 3in (75mm) diameter plastic-canvas circles

Anchor Stranded Floss
  four skeins: 118 iris
  one skein: 926 cream

7 x 4in (180 x 100mm) lightweight cotton or cotton blend lining fabric

7 x 4in (180 x 100mm) heavyweight interfacing

From the plastic canvas, cut one side piece 35 x 9 bars, one lining 31 x 9 bars, and one hinge 14 x 3 bars.

Use twelve strands of floss for the satin, tent, and edge stitch, and six elsewhere.

CROWN LINING

Leaving the first and last four bars of the plastic canvas uncovered, work alternating lines of tent and satin stitch in cream across the hat lining (31 x 9).

Overlap the uncovered ends, right side facing in, matching the bars, and baste. Complete the embroidery through both layers, joining into a ring. Edge stitch both edges.

SIDE

Leaving the first and last four bars of the plastic canvas uncovered, work a line of tent stitch down one long edge of the side canvas (35 x 9) in cream stranded floss. Next work a line of sloping satin stitch over three bars, and another line of tent stitch. Then work a line of long cross stitch in iris. Overlap and complete through both layers.

HINGE

Work a central line of tent stitch in iris, then overcast all around the outer edge.

CIRCLES

For the base, starting at the outer edge, cover one circle as follows:

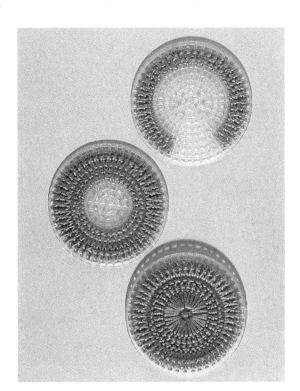

FIG. 21 Base, brim, and crown of hatbox

1) a line of tied cross stitch over three bars next to the edge
2) a round of straight stitch over one bar
3) a round of cross stitch
4) satin stitch into the center, using six strands
5) a cross stitch over the center intersection

Work rounds of the backstitch between the lines of stitching where necessary to fill in and completely cover. Finally, edge stitch all around.

For the brim, work rounds 1, 2, and 3 as above on another circle. Leaving one bar beside the embroidery, carefully cut out the center of the circle. Edge stitch around the outer edge of the brim.

For the crown, embroider a cross at the center of the third circle, surrounded by satin stitch over two bars. Cut out, leaving one bar outside the embroidery. Keep the outer part of the circle intact, as it will be used as a guide for cutting the interfacing and lining. Back stitch between the outer bar and the embroidery.

TO FINISH

Overcast the hat crown to the hat side. Place the hat side in position over the brim, with un-covered edges matching, and overcast in place using twelve strands of cream stranded floss.

Cut one bar from the outer edge of the frame circle left after cutting the hat crown. Cut two circles of interfacing the same size, but without the hole at the center. Cut two circles of lining fabric, adding ⅝in (15mm) seam allowance all around.

Place one piece of lining fabric right side down with a piece of interfacing centered on top. Turn the edges over and baste using small stitches, smoothing the edge as you go. Slip stitch the lining to the hat base using three strands of iris stranded floss. Remove the basting.

Using the plastic-canvas circle as a guide, mark the central hole with a lead pencil on the second piece of interfacing. Cut out the center. Cover the interfacing with lining as above. Clip the exposed fabric at the center and carefully clip at intervals to the edge of the interfacing.

Slip stitch the lining under the hat brim around the outer edge, pushing the spare fabric at the center into the crown. Slip the embroidered lining into the hat, pushing the spare lining smoothly inside. There is no need to stitch.

Overcast the hinge to the hat base and brim using three strands of iris floss.

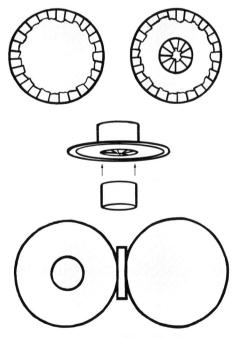

FIG. 22 Assembly of hatbox

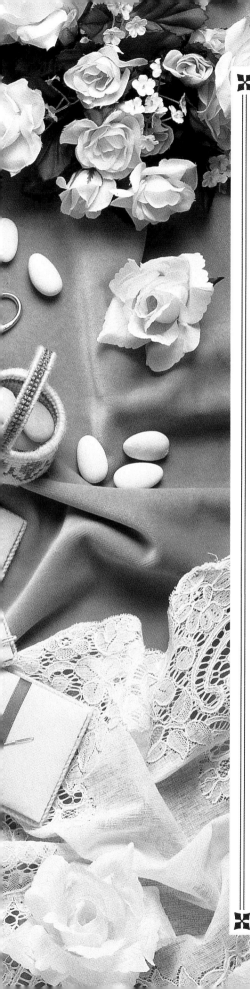

– 3 –
Victorian-style Boxes

$\mathcal{P}$LASTIC canvas really comes into its own when making boxes. Because it requires no seam allowances, construction is very easy. To make the box completely washable, ultra-stiff canvas may be used instead of cardboard for the lining.

The boxes in this chapter are based on Victorian designs, although the originals were usually covered in paper and often had photographs inset. The sides are hinged to the base so that they fall open when the lid is removed, affording easy access to the contents.

Although they may look complicated, they are actually very easy to make. The secret of success lies in making the cardboard lining just the right size, so that when the box is closed, the sides fit together neatly without bulging.

Mini basket, square sewing box, pin box, and dressing table box

Square Sewing Box

This box uses plastic canvas for the main structure and fabric-covered cardboard for the lining, and has a matching pin box and mini basket. The design could easily be reduced or enlarged to make other sizes, or stitched in light colors on a dark background to give a completely different effect.

MATERIALS

10 x 9in (250 x 230mm) plastic canvas, 10 bars
   per inch (25mm)
36 x 3½in (900 x 90mm) lining fabric
17 x 3in (400 x 80mm) batting
7in (180mm) square of medium-weight cardboard
8 x 7in (200 x 180mm) lightweight cardboard
20in (500mm) of ¼in (5mm) wide ribbon
Clear glue
Paterna Stranded Yarn
   seven skeins: 263 cream
Anchor Pearl Cotton No. 5
   three skeins each of: 216 green; 895 pink
   one skein: 305 yellow

From the plastic canvas, for the outer box, cut one base 27 x 27 bars, four sides 30 x 27 bars, one lid 29 x 29 bars, and four lid sides 29 x 7 bars. For the inner box, cut one base 12 x 12 bars and four sides 22 x 12 bars. For the thimble box, cut five pieces 9 x 9 bars. From the medium cardboard, cut four sides 2¾ x 2⅜in (70 x 63mm). From the lightweight cardboard, cut four inner box sides 2 x ¹⁵⁄₁₆in (50 x 24mm), two base pieces 2½in (64mm) square, and one inner lid 2¾in (70mm) square.

Use pearl cotton singly for the cross stitch, doubled for tent stitch. Use a single strand of yarn for the small cross stitch and two strands elsewhere. Embroider following the charts.

PREPARING THE LINING

Using the cardboard as a guide, cut out the lining fabric, allowing ⅝in (15mm) extra all around. Cut out eight pieces of batting the same size as the heavier cardboard sides.

Place a piece of lining fabric right side down on a flat surface with the batting centered over it and the cardboard on top. Trim the corners. Spread glue evenly along the edges of the cardboard. Fold over the allowances and press into place all around, pulling the fabric taut to avoid wrinkles on the right side. Inset the allowances at the corners to make sure they will not show later. Place a heavy book or other flat object on top and let the glue set. Line the other cardboard pieces in the same way.

Cut the ribbon to the width of each cardboard side, plus ½in (13mm) allowances. Place rib-

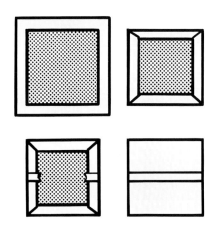

FIG. 23 Lining of square sewing box

bon across the center of each side lining and glue the surplus in place on the back.

TO MAKE THE SEWING BOX

Using the cream yarn, edge stitch the sides and upper edges of the eight embroidered box sides.

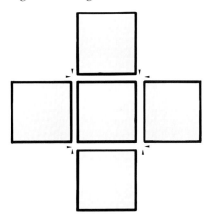

FIG. 24 Stitching up the square sewing box

FIG. 25 Gluing the square sewing box

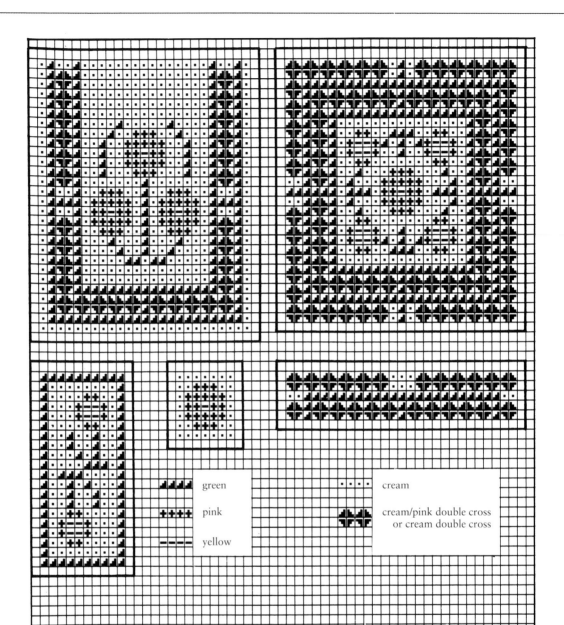

Square sewing box

Place the lower edge of one large side section against the box base, wrong sides facing and edges matching up. Join with edge stitch to form a hinge. Repeat with the other three sides.

Attach the inner box sides to the inner box base in the same way, but with the wrong side of the sides against the right side of base.

Overcast the four sides of the thimble box to the thimble box base, with the wrong side of the sides against right side of base. Join the corners and overcast around the top edge.

Edge stitch the lid sides to the lid, and join the corners. Overcast all around the lower edge, matching the colors of the embroidery. Glue the prepared lining sections in position on the inside lid and on both sides of the base. The edges of the lining should lie against the inside of the edge stitch. Glue the lining sections to the inside of the box sides.

Glue the thimble box to the inner box base. Glue the inner box to the box base, placing it at a diagonal to the outer box base as shown.

Pin Box and Mini Basket

This little pin box and mini basket are designed to complement the Square Sewing Box in a matching set. The pin box is divided into two: one section is a padded pincushion; the other holds loose pins. The deep lid fits over both. The basket makes use of the circle of plastic canvas left over when the pin box lid is cut out.

MATERIALS

PIN BOX

9 x 4in (230 x 100mm) plastic canvas, 10 bars
   per inch (25mm)
Three 3in (75mm) diameter plastic-canvas circles
6 x 4in (150 x 100mm) cotton canvas, 14 threads
   per inch (25mm)
12 x 3½in (200 x 90mm) lining fabric
9 x 3in (230 x 75mm) batting
6in (150mm) square of cardboard

MINI BASKET

7 x 3in (175 x 75mm) plastic canvas, 10 bars
   per inch (25mm)
3in (75mm) diameter plastic-canvas circle with
   three bars cut from the outer edge

FOR BOTH ITEMS

Paterna Stranded Yarn
   five skeins: 263 cream
Anchor Pearl Cotton No. 5
   two skeins each of: 895 pink; 216 green
   a small amount of: 305 yellow
Sewing thread to match the lining

PIN BOX

From the plastic canvas, cut one box side 92 x 10 bars, one inner box side 83 x 9 bars, one backing strip 8 x 10 bars and another 8 x 9 bars, one divider 24 x 9 bars.

Use a single strand of yarn or pearl cotton for the cross stitch and edge stitch on the 10-bar plastic canvas. Use the same yarn or cotton doubled for edge stitching around the circle and for the overcasting.

Baste the 8 x 10 backing strip to the right end of the plastic canvas side (88 x 10),

underlapping it by four bars (Fig. 3, page 14). Leaving the first and last four bars uncovered, work the embroidery from the chart. Lap the left end over the backing strip and complete the embroidery through both layers, joining into a ring (Fig. 4, page 14). Embroider the inner box side in the same way. Embroider the box divider, overcasting the short edges.

For the box top, using the pearl cotton doubled, work a line of cross stitch next to the outer bar of one circle. Alternate green and pink stitches. Cut out the center of this circle to make a frame, leaving one bar beside the embroidery. Overcast the inner edge in cream.

Cut one bar off the edge of another plastic-canvas circle and cut in half. Leaving three bars all around, cut out a semicircular opening from one of the sections for the pincushion. Work cross stitch in alternating green and pink. Overcast the inner edge in cream.

Embroider the cotton canvas following the chart on page 42, making sure the embroidery fills the frame for the top. Embroider an area of cotton canvas in cream tent stitch to fill the semicircular opening.

PREPARING THE LINING

Cut three circles of cardboard just a little smaller than the plastic-canvas circle, so that the edge comes halfway between the two outer bars. Cover two circles with fabric; set the third aside.

Cut three circles of batting, one the size of the lid embroidery, one slightly smaller, and another smaller still.

TO MAKE THE PIN BOX

Press the canvas from the wrong side. Trim all

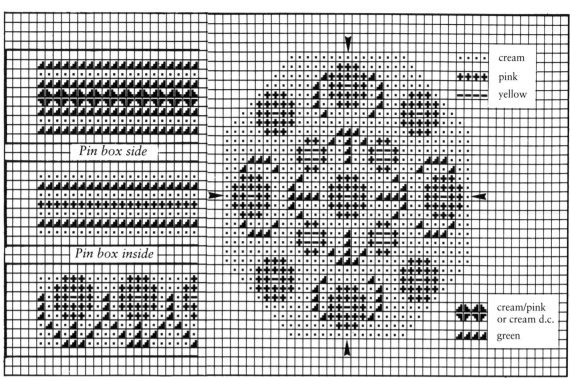

Pin box side

Pin box inside

cream
pink
yellow

cream/pink
or cream d.c.
green

Mini basket

Cotton-canvas pin box top

around so that the edge is just inside the outer edge of the prepared plastic-canvas frame. Glue sparingly around the wrong side of the frame and place it carefully over the embroidery. Ease the cotton canvas up slightly to allow for the doming effect when it is padded. The circle of flowers around the outer edge should be just visible. Hold the frame in position until set. Overcast the embroidered lid to the box side. Overcast around the lower edge.

Center the circles of batting in order of size on the wrong side of one fabric-covered cardboard circle, smallest first. Glue all around the outer edge. Press into position inside the pin box lid, and hold until set. The batting should make the canvas dome slightly. Glue the pincushion cotton canvas in position in

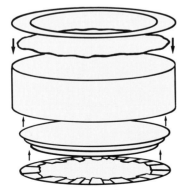

FIG. 26 Assembly of the pin box

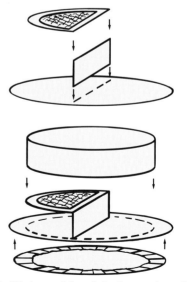

FIG. 27 Assembly of the base of pin box

Mini basket and pin box

the half-circle frame, and hold until set.

Place the divider across the center of a circle of plastic canvas and stitch into position using cream yarn. Overcast the inner box side to the base, taking the stitching over the bar next to the edge. Using matching sewing thread, stitch the second covered cardboard circle to the underside of the base. Place the embroidered half circle in position over one half and overcast into place, stuffing with batting before completing. Continue the stitching to overcast the other half section. Cut the remaining cardboard circle in half, and trim as necessary to fit the pin box. Cover with lining fabric and slip into place to complete. Overcast the edge.

MINI BASKET

From the plastic canvas, cut one side 68 x 10 bars, one lining 62 x 9 bars, and one handle 54 x 4 bars.

Make the mini basket following the instructions in Chapter 1 (pages 12–13) for the Circular Basket, following the chart opposite.

Dressing Table Box

This box is made in a manner similar to that of the sewing box, but the lid sides lie flush with the sides of the box when closed. The central box is designed to hold spare buttons together with needles and thread for emergency repairs. The inside of the pin box is padded, so it can be used as a pincushion. The small compartments of this useful box would make it equally suitable for storing jewelry.

It is best to decide what you wish to keep in the box before cutting out the plastic canvas so that the compartments can be cut to size. The small side pockets at the center of the long sides are designed to support the sides when the box is closed. If you wish to store large items, these could be omitted to give extra space.

MATERIALS

One 14 x 11in (355 x 280mm) sheet of plastic canvas, 10 bars per inch (25mm)
18 x 7in (450 x 180mm) lining fabric
8 x 6in (200 x 150mm) batting
6 x 5in (150 x 125mm) medium-weight cardboard
11 x 6in (280 x 150mm) lightweight cardboard
36in (900mm) of ⅛in (3mm) wide ribbon
Clear glue
Paterna Stranded Yarn
  four skeins: 494 flesh
Anchor Pearl Cotton No. 5
  four skeins: 896 dark pink
  one skein each of: 894 medium pink; 893 light pink; 216 green; 305 yellow

From the plastic canvas, for the outer box, cut a base and lid 57 x 33 bars each, two sides 57 x 13 bars and two sides 33 x 13 bars, two lid sides 57 x 7 bars and two lid sides 33 x 7 bars. For the inner box, cut two sides 51 x 10 bars and two sides 21 x 10 bars, two dividers 20 x 10 bars and one 10 x 10 bars, two outer pockets 19 x 10 bars and four 3 x 10 bars. For the thimble boxes, cut ten pieces 9 x 9 bars. For the pin box lid, cut a lid and lid facing 21 x 21 bars each, one underlid 17 x 17 bars, and four lid sides 17 x 4 bars.

Use pearl cotton singly and two strands of yarn. For the cardboard pieces, see "Preparing the Lining" on page 46.

OUTER BOX

For the sides, using the dark pink pearl cotton, start at the top left corner with a small cross stitch and then work ten long cross stitches diagonally down to the right. Continue in zigzag

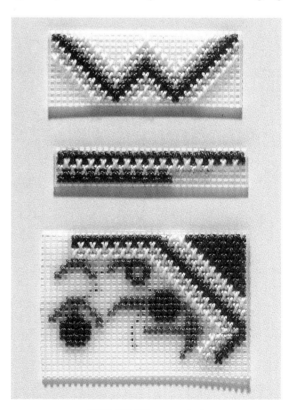

FIG. 28 Zigzag stitch

Dressing table box

as shown in the photograph, finishing with a small cross stitch. On each side of this line work a line in light pink, then one in flesh yarn. Fill in the triangles with dark pink. Work edge stitch around the sides and the top edge in dark pink. For the long sides start as shown, working three complete zigzags.

For the lid sides, work a line in long cross stitch in dark pink, then one in light pink, one in flesh yarn, and finally a line in dark pink.

For the lid, work the corners in long cross stitch using the photograph as a guide. Embroider the floral center in small cross stitch, following the chart on page 46.

INNER BOX

For the box base, work a border in tent stitch with flesh yarn.

For the inside box, embroider the long sides following the flower border chart. Work the two

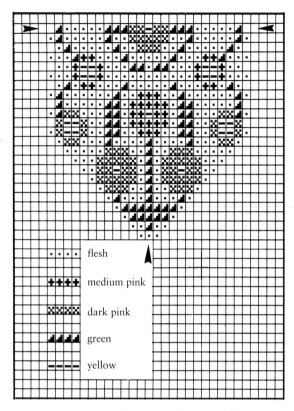

Center of dressing table box lid

· · · ·	flesh
+ + + +	medium pink
⬛⬛⬛⬛	dark pink
◢◢◢◢	green
= = = =	yellow

board, cut a lid and outer base 5½ x 3in (140 x 76mm) each, four pieces 1⅞ x ⅞in (48 x 22mm) and four pieces 1¹³⁄₁₆ x ⅞in (46 x 22mm), and two pieces 1¹³⁄₁₆in (46mm) square.

Line the four pieces of heavier cardboard for the outer sides as for the Square Sewing Box. Because the box lining extends above the embroidered side, the seam allowance at the top needs to be deep enough to give a neat finish. Add strips of ribbon across the center of each piece.

Line the lighter cardboard for the lid and the outer base and the eight pieces of cardboard for the inner compartments. Cut a piece of lining fabric 1⅝in (40mm) square for the pincushion.

TO MAKE THE BOX

Slip stitch a section of lined cardboard to the lid. Edge stitch the lid pieces into a box shape, then edge stitch all around the lower edge with dark pink.

Overcast the outer pocket sides (10 x 3) to the inner box sides over the uncovered bars of plastic canvas. Overcast the sides to the base over the bar next to the tent stitch and join the corners. Overcast the outer pockets to the base and join the corners. Overcast the dividers in place.

Stitch the thimble sections into two box shapes of five squares each and place in position in the smaller compartment of the inner box. Edge stitch the top edges, joining the thimble boxes as you go. Slip stitch the lined cardboard to the outer base.

Glue the prepared box linings in place, longer ones first, and slip in the base linings.

Place one pin box underlid side against the lid facing, with one long edge against the bar next to the tent stitch. Overcast to join. Repeat with the other three sides. Join the four corners to make a shallow box shape. Place the pin box lid on top of the underlid, with wrong sides facing, and edge stitch in dark pink to join.

Spread glue evenly around the inside of the prepared underlid frame. Place pincushion lining fabric centrally on the frame and let it set, easing out fabric to avoid wrinkles. This could be stitched in place if preferred. Edge stitch the frame section to the lid, stuffing with batting before completing the stitching.

Edge stitch the box sides to the base. To complete the box, glue the box side linings in place.

short sides and the outer pockets with two flower shapes. Start at the center and work out, covering the extra bar at each end of the short sides with cross stitch. Work a line of tent stitch to cover the four outer pocket sides.

For the dividers and thimble boxes, cover each piece with tent stitch in light pink pearl cotton.

Cover the four pin box lid sides (17 x 4) with tent stitch in flesh yarn. Embroider the pin box lid (21 x 21) following the chart opposite. Work a line of tent stitch in flesh yarn around the edge of the second square (21 x 21).

Work a line in dark pink pearl cotton around the outer edge of the underlid square (17 x 17). Cut away the central uncovered area, leaving one bar beside the embroidery to form a frame. Edge stitch this inner edge in flesh yarn.

PREPARING THE LINING

From the medium-weight cardboard, cut two pieces 5½ x 1½in (138 x 38mm) and two pieces 3 x 1½in (76 x 38mm). From the lighter card-

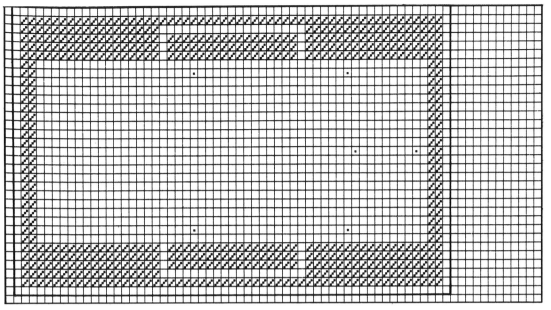

(above) Base of dressing table box   (below) Dressing table box interior

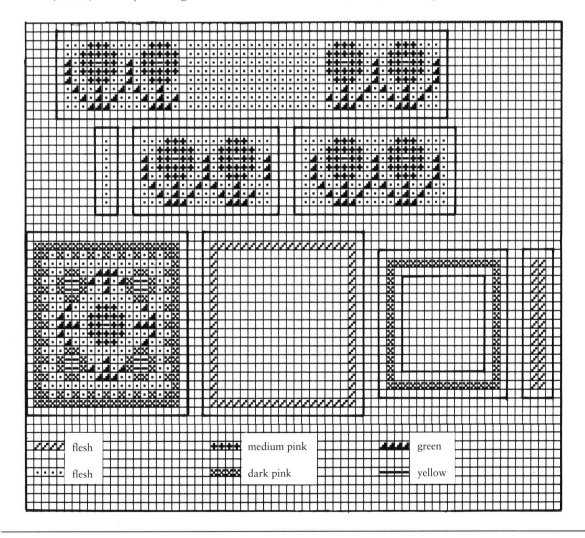

| | flesh | | medium pink | | green |
| | flesh | | dark pink | | yellow |

– 4 –
Embroidered Boxes

*Y*ou can make many shapes or sizes of box using the ultra-stiff plastic canvas now available. It can be used for the outer box, or as a stiff lining to give rigidity, as in the circular box shown here. However, the ultra-stiff canvas is not suitable for making very small circular boxes, as it will snap when bent into a tight ring.

The patterns for boxes shown here could be easily adapted to different sizes. For instance, 7-bar plastic canvas could be substituted for 10-bar canvas, and larger circles could be used for the circular box, adapting the embroidery design as necessary.

Once you have mastered the art of box making, it is relatively simple to adapt the method for making the box in a natural fabric if this is preferred. The embroidered sections would need to be stretched around cardboard before assembling.

Very small boxes do not need to be lined, but you should take extra care to keep the inside neat, and you should assemble them with the right side of the base inside the box. When lining a box with cardboard, you should choose the right thickness for the box. While lightweight cardboard is suitable for very small boxes, medium-weight cardboard gives a good rigid finish for larger ones.

Fitted circular box, travel sewing box, three nesting boxes, and gold initial box

Fitted Circular Box

For a different effect, stitching with ribbon gives a lovely rich look to the texture of the embroidery. For maximum sheen, the ribbon should lie flat on the surface.

This box is a decorative way of keeping essential sewing items at hand. Keep one in your living room, and you will never be without access to a needle and thread.

MATERIALS

6in (150mm) square of cotton canvas, 12 threads
    per inch (25mm)
14 x 4in (355 x 100mm) plastic canvas, 10 bars
    per inch (25mm)
13 x 6in (330 x 150mm) ultra-stiff plastic canvas,
    7 bars per inch (25mm)
Four 4¼in (110mm) diameter plastic-canvas
    circles
Lightweight cotton or cotton blend lining
    fabric, bias cut
    one piece 13¼ x 3¼in (335 x 80mm)
    one piece 15 x 15in (380 x 125mm)
16 x 8in (400 x 200mm) of batting
15 x 5in (380 x 125mm) lightweight cardboard
Clear glue
Anchor Pearl Cotton No. 5
    five skeins: 400 charcoal
    one skein: 398 light gray
Anchor Stranded Floss
    five skeins: 387 cream
    two skeins: 860 green
⅝in (15mm wide) Offray ribbon
    3¼yd (3m) of 168 colonial rose
    4⅜yd (4m) of 447 iris
    3¾yd (3.5mm) of 660 yellow
Sewing thread to match the lining fabric

From the 10-bar plastic canvas, cut one side 132
x 23 bars and one backing strip 8 x 23 bars. From
the 7-bar plastic canvas, cut one lining piece 89
x 13 bars, one lid rim 85 x 3 bars, one tray support 85 x 6 bars, one tray side 82 x 6 bars, one
tray divider 25 x 6 bars and one 13 x 6 bars.
From the batting, cut one piece 7 x 3½in (180 x
90mm), and put the remainder aside.

Use pearl cotton doubled for the embroidery
and singly when working the edge stitch on the
10-bar plastic canvas. Use twelve strands of the
stranded floss.

THE SIDE

For details on sewing with ribbon, see Chapter
11, page 117.

Baste the backing strip (8 x 23) to the right
end of the side piece of plastic canvas (132 x
23), underlapping it by four bars. Leaving four
bars uncovered at each end, work the embroidery from the example. Lap the left end over

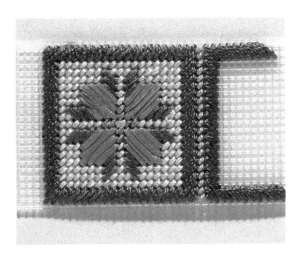

FIG. 29 Ribbon box side pattern

the right to form a ring and complete the embroidery through both layers.

THE LID

Work a line of tent stitch in light gray pearl cotton over the bar next to the edge of one plastic-
canvas circle. Very carefully cut out the inner
uncovered area, taking care to leave one bar
inside the stitching. Trim off the spikes and edge
stitch in charcoal pearl cotton. Work a line of
tent stitch in charcoal over the bar next to the
edge of a second circle.

Leaving the first and last four bars uncovered, work a line of tent stitch in charcoal along
the lid rim (85 x 3) bars. Overlap the ends and
complete the stitching through both layers.

Work the embroidery on the cotton canvas,
filling in the cream background as necessary to
fill the opening when the frame is placed over it.

THE INTERIOR

For the tray support, leaving the first and last
four bars uncovered, embroider the strip of plastic canvas (85 x 6) with four lines of tent stitch
in charcoal pearl cotton. Overlap the four bars
at each end and complete the embroidery
through both layers to join into a ring. Edge
stitch both edges.

For the tray side and dividers, embroider the
tray side in the same way as the support, working a line of tent stitch in light gray pearl cotton
along the upper edge. Embroider the dividers,
overcasting the short ends as you go.

FIG. 30 Embroidery on cotton canvas

THE LINING

Overlap the plastic canvas for the lining (89 x 13) by four bars, matching up the holes, and baste securely in place. Baste the strip of batting to the inside, trimming it to butt the edges to avoid bulk. Trim the edges of the batting even with the plastic canvas.

FIG. 31 Overlapping the side

Join the lining fabric into a ring, taking a ½in (13mm) seam. Place this INSIDE the plastic canvas, wrong side against the batting. Fold the upper seam allowance to the outside and baste in place. The joining seam may be adjusted at this point, if necessary. Turn the lower allowance to the outside and baste. Work herringbone stitch between the folded edges to hold them in place. Remove the basting.

Cut two cardboard circles slightly smaller than the plastic-canvas circles. The edge should be between the outer bar and the one next to it, to allow the needle to pass through when stitching. Cover one cardboard circle with lining fabric and one with batting and lining fabric.

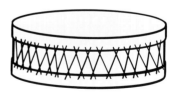

FIG. 32 Box lining

Cut two bars off the outer edge of one circle of plastic canvas. Cut three circles of cardboard slightly smaller than this, as before. Cover one circle with lining and one with lining and batting. The third will be used to line the tray.

THE UNDERLID

Overcast the rim to the plastic-canvas circle with the charcoal edge, taking the stitches over the bar next to the tent stitch. As there are more holes on the circle than on the rim, you will need to work two stitches into one hole at intervals. Overcast the free edge.

Using the matching sewing thread, slip stitch the smaller covered cardboard circle with the batting inside the underlid.

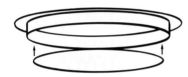

FIG. 33 Underlid preparation

THE UPPER LID

Place the frame with the light gray tent stitch over the prepared embroidery and trim the canvas so that the edge is just inside the outer edge of the plastic canvas. Glue sparingly around the underside of the frame and place the embroidery in position behind it. Ease the canvas up slightly to allow for the dome effect when it is padded. The four flowers should be just visible. Hold in position until set.

Cut a circle of batting the size of the lid embroidery, another one slightly smaller, and another one smaller still. Place the underlid on the table, wrong side up. Center the smaller piece of batting over it, followed by the other two in order of size. Place the embroidered lid over the top and edge stitch all around in charcoal to join them. The batting should make the canvas dome slightly.

TO MAKE THE BOX

For the box, slip stitch the larger covered circle of cardboard without batting to a plastic-canvas circle. Place this, lining side down, with the box side over it, and edge stitch all around to join them, using charcoal pearl cotton. Edge stitch around the box side top in charcoal.

Spread glue inside the box, close to the upper edge. Slip the prepared lining into position. Place clothespins or paper clips all around the edge to hold firmly until set. Slip in the second lined circle, followed by the tray support.

For the tray, place the longer divider on the trimmed plastic-canvas circle, with the edge against the straight bar across the center to divide it in half. The line of light gray stitching should be along the upper edge. Overcast the divider in place along the base. Repeat with the shorter piece, dividing one half into quarters.

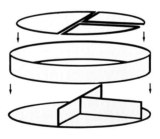

FIG. 35 Tray

Slip stitch the smaller lined circle without the batting to the underside of the tray. Place the prepared side over this, and overcast the edges together with charcoal to form the tray. Edge stitch all around, catching in the top of the dividers as you go, then edge stitch the dividers in charcoal.

Cut the remaining cardboard circle to fit these divisions, cover with lining fabric, and place in the tray. Slip the tray into the box; it is now ready to be filled with your sewing things.

FIG. 34 Lid preparation

Gold Initial Box

The embroidery for this box is worked using stranded floss and a gold ribbon-type thread in a mixture of smooth satin stitch and chunky Rhodes stitch. To give the design extra sparkle, the initial is also out-lined with beads. The variation in light and shadow is obtained by working the satin stitch blocks in alternate directions.

MATERIALS

10 x 9in (250 x 225mm) plastic canvas, 10 bars per inch (25mm)

Two pieces 4⅝ x 4in (112 x 102mm) lightweight cardboard

13 x 5in (330 x 125mm) medium-weight cardboard

36 x 6in (900 x 150mm) soft cotton or cotton blend lining fabric

1oz (30g) gold beads

Fine needle for beading

Matching sewing thread

Clear glue

Anchor Stranded Floss
  seven skeins: 386 cream

Three spools of gold Diadem metallic thread

From the plastic canvas, cut a lid and base 46 x 42 bars each, two sides 46 x 18 and two 42 x 18 bars. From the lighter cardboard, cut an outer base and lid lining 4⅜ x 4in (111 x 100m). From the medium cardboard, cut one lid lining 4⅛ x 3¾in (105 x 95mm), one inner base 4¼ x 3⅞in (108 x 98mm), two sides 4⅜ x 1⅝in (111 x 42mm), and two sides 3⅞ x 1⅝in (98 x 40mm).

Use nine strands of floss for the satin stitch squares and six strands for edge stitching. Use a single strand of the gold thread.

First work the border of Rhodes stitch around the lid (46 x 42). Work an extra stitch inside each corner.

Embroider your chosen initial (see chart page 56) in Rhodes stitch in the center. Fill in with satin stitch blocks worked in alternate directions, using stranded floss.

Work straight stitch in gold between the satin stitch squares and around the initial, omitting the edges of the lid.

STITCHING WITH BEADS

To bead the embroidered initial, choose a needle, such as a long, fine beading needle, that will pass through the hole in the beads.

Place some of the beads in a shallow dish. Thread the needle with the sewing thread and fasten securely behind the top left corner of the intial. Bring the needle through to the right side. Pick up several beads on the point of the needle and slide them down to touch the embroidery. Continue until you have about 1in (25mm) of beads on the thread. Take the needle through to the back and work several back stitches. Next move back to the left, taking a stitch between every few beads to couch the thread down at intervals. Outline the initial and then work beading between the Rhodes stitches.

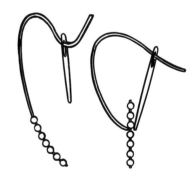

FIG. 36 Beading

TO MAKE THE BOX

See Chapter 11 (pages 117–18) for more details on making a box with an attached lid.

Cover the thinner cardboard with lining and the remaining cardboard with lining and batting. Slip stitch one thin piece of cardboard to the base (46 x 42). This will be the outer base.

Omitting the edge above the letter, edge stitch around three sides of the lid. Glue the second thin piece of cardboard to the wrong side of the lid. Glue the padded lining to the center.

Edge stitch the box sides to the base and join the corners. Edge stitch around three sides of the top edge, two short and one long. Edge stitch the lid to the box section.

Gold initial box and travel sewing box

Glue the two longer side lining sections into the box at the back and front. Repeat for the short sides. These fit between the longer lining sections. Slip the base lining inside, and your box is complete.

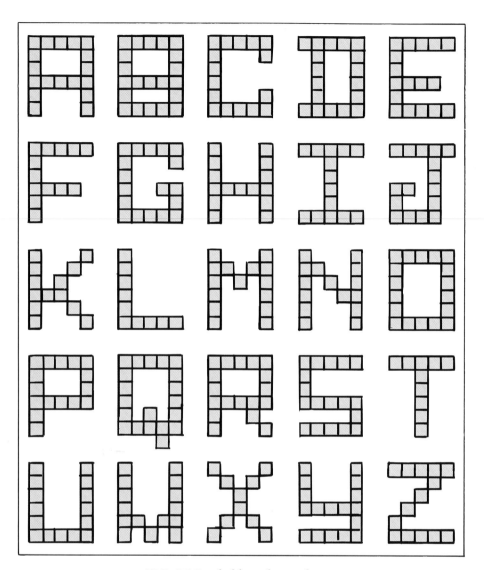

FIG. 37 Beaded box: letter chart

MAKING A TASSEL

Decide which thread or mixture of threads you wish to use and wind a quantity around three fingers. Slip the loops off. This will now be referred to as the tassel.

Take a length of thread, about 18in (450mm) long, double it, and slip the folded end through the tassel, taking the ends through the loop and pulling tight. Thread both ends into the tapestry needle and stitch to the center of the opening side of the box lid.

Wrap the thread around the tassel, about ¼in (6mm) down, and make a knot or two to secure the head. Take the ends down through the center of the tassel and let them join the loop. Cut the loop and trim it to a suitable length.

FIG. 38 Tassel

Travel Sewing Box

This small, shallow box can be lined with thin cardboard, which helps to keep it lightweight.

MATERIALS

9 x 6in (225 x 150mm) plastic canvas, 10 bars per inch (25mm)

9 x 6in (225 x 150mm) lightweight cardboard

16 x 6in (400 x 150mm) lining fabric

⅜in (10mm) diameter button

Anchor Pearl Cotton No. 5
   two skeins: 77 pink

⅝in (15mm) wide Offray ribbon
   10yd (9m) of 815 cream
   17yd (15.5m) of 275 wine

From the plastic canvas, cut a lid and base 42 x 42 bars each, and four sides 42 x 6 bars. From lightweight cardboard, cut two lid pieces 3¹⁵⁄₁₆in (99mm) square, two sides 4 x ⅜in (100 x 10mm), and two sides 3¹⁵⁄₁₆ x ⅜in (99 x 10mm).

Use the pearl cotton doubled for the embroidery, singly for the edge stitch.

Work the embroidery following Fig. 39, referring to Chapter 11 for working with ribbon. For maximum effect the ribbon should lie flat on the surface. Stitch the button to the center of one side. Finish as for the Gold Initial Box, omitting the second piece of lined cardboard on the lid. Make a buttonhole loop with a tassel at the center front of the lid.

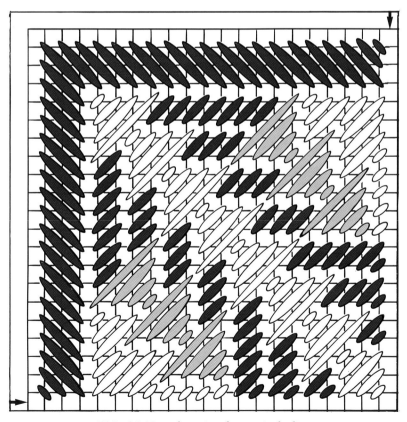

FIG. 39 Travel sewing box: stitch diagram

Three Nesting Boxes

These boxes are worked in a mixture of ribbon and stranded floss. Each box fits snugly into the next. They are not lined, so it is important to keep the embroidery on the inside as neat as possible. The quantities specified are enough to make all three boxes. The chart for the flower pattern is on page 52, Fig. 30.

One 14 x 11in (355 x 280mm) sheet of plastic
   canvas, 10 bars per inch (25mm)
⅝in (15mm) wide Offray ribbon
   9yd (8m) of 168 colonial rose
   20yd (18m) of 447 iris
   2¼yd (2m) of 660 yellow gold
Anchor Stranded Floss
   nine skeins: 387 cream
   two skeins each of: 305 yellow; 118 iris;
   860 green
   one skein: 77 pink

From the plastic canvas, for the small box, cut
one lid 17 x 17 bars, four lid sides 17 x 6 bars,
one base 15 x 15 bars, and four base sides 15 x
5 bars. For the medium box, cut one lid 21 x
21 bars, four lid sides 21 x 8 bars, one base 19
x 19 bars, and four base sides 19 x 7 bars. For
the large box, cut one lid 25 x 25 bars, four lid
sides 25 x 10 bars, one base 23 x 23 bars, and
four base sides 23 x 9 bars.

   Use twelve strands of floss for the embroidery and six for the edge stitch.

LARGE BOX

Work a single line of tent stitch in cream next
to the outer edge of the square lid piece. Next
work satin stitch in iris ribbon over two bars.
As you work each stitch, hold the ribbon between finger and thumb and guide it through
the canvas to keep it flat. (See Chapter 11 for
further details of sewing with ribbon.) Fill in
with the center pattern from the example shown
in Fig. 30.

   Work a line of tent stitch in cream around
the outer edge of each side piece. Next work a
line of satin stitch over two bars in iris ribbon.
Fill in with satin stitch in yellow stranded floss.

   Work the base in the same way as the lid,
omitting the cream tent stitch around the edges.

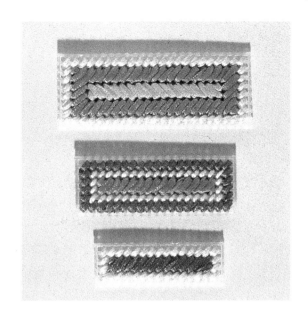

FIG. 40 *Sides of the three nesting boxes*

MEDIUM BOX

Work a single line of tent stitch in pink ribbon
around the outer edge of the lid. Fill in the center
pattern following Fig. 30.

   Work a line of tent stitch in pink ribbon next
to the edge of the four sides. Next work a line
in cream. Fill in with iris stranded floss.

   Work the base in the same way, omitting the
pink tent stitch around the outer edges.

SMALL BOX

Embroider the lid following Fig. 30, omitting
the square of cream tent stitch around the edge.
Work tent stitch in cream around the edge of
the side. Fill in with satin stitch in pink ribbon.

   Work the base as for the lid, omitting one
line of the pattern at the edges.

TO MAKE THE BOXES

See Chapter 11, pages 117-18, for details of how
to stitch the boxes and lids together.

– 5 –
Country Cottage Desk Accessories

*T*HIS detailed model of a country cottage is in fact a desk accessory complete with pen holder and small shelves. The large sloping roof lifts to reveal the interior.

I first saw a picture of "Corner Thatch" in a book of English cottages, looking for all the world like a tiny doll's house. It was built as a barn in the late seventeenth century and was later converted to a cottage. The contrast in color and texture between the walls and the thatched roof, with the tiny splash of red in the mailbox, just asked to be reproduced in some form of embroidery.

The stitched address-book cover and stamp holder are worked in the same black, white, and red to team with the cottage design.

A model could be made of any house or cottage, though most buildings will need simplifying. It is important to decide on the salient features of the building, and then work out the size from these. I wanted my model of the cottage to be approximately to scale, and small enough to fit in my living room as a decorative feature. The main difficulty was keeping the size down while retaining the essential details.

Desk accessories

The Cottage

The windows are the main feature of the front, so I started with these, working a sample to decide how many bars of 10-bar plastic canvas would be needed to get enough detail. The wooden sections were then calculated in proportion to the windows. The same method was used for the side walls. The resulting model is 10½ x 10 x 8in high (265 x 250 x 200mm). The ends of the roof were omitted to allow easy opening of the box lid.

MATERIALS

Five 14 x 11in (355 x 280mm) sheets of plastic
  canvas, 10 bars per inch (25mm)
23 x 20in (585 x 510mm) medium-weight
  cardboard for lining
10½ x 7¾in (266 x 197mm) lightweight
  cardboard for inner lining
18 x 12in (460 x 300mm) lightweight velvet
  jersey for lining
9⅝ x ⅜ x ⅛in (240 x 10 x 3mm) peice of wood
Curved sewing needle
Clear glue
Paterna Stranded Yarn
  twenty skeins: 220 black
  ten skeins: 263 cream
  eight skeins: 200 dark gray
  seven skeins: 471 brown
  one skein: 950 red
Anchor Stranded Floss
  two skeins each of 400 charcoal; 926 cream
  one skein each of 896 pink; 388 beige

THE BUILDING

Two 18 x 12in (460 x 310mm) sheets ultra-stiff
  plastic canvas, 7 bars per inch (25mm)
17 x 10in (400 x 250mm) 2mm cardboard

From the 10-bar plastic canvas, for the walls
and floor, cut one front wall 97 x 43 bars, one
back wall 97 x 20 bars, two side walls 79 x 76
bars, and one floor 97 x 79 bars.

For the bay window, cut one piece 23 x 14
bars, two pieces 17 x 5 bars, two bay supports
12 x 3 bars.

For the eaves, cut four pieces 78 x 3 bars,
two pieces 78 x 5 bars, four pieces 98 x 3 bars,
two pieces 98 x 5 bars, four pieces 46 x 3 bars,
and two pieces 46 x 5 bars.

For the mailbox, cut one piece 32 x 12 bars,
two pieces 12 x 8 bars, two pieces 12 x 3 bars,
two pieces 27 x 6 bars, and one piece 12 x 6 bars.

For the main roof, cut one piece 107 x 80 bars
and one piece 107 x 56 bars. For the roof edges,
cut two pieces 107 x 3 bars, two pieces 80 x 3
bars, and two pieces 56 x 3 bars. Cut two roof
coping pieces 107 x 8 bars, one roof ridge 107 x
6 bars, and two gable ends 30 x 15 bars.

From the ultra-stiff mesh, for the shelves, cut
two 62 x 32 bars, two 62 x 14 bars, and two
sides 31 x 33 bars. For the pen holder, cut one
base 89 x 20 bars, one front 89 x 7 bars, and
two sides 17 x 7 bars.

Use two strands of yarn unless otherwise
stated. Use twelve strands of stranded floss.

WALLS AND WINDOWS

Work the four walls in tent stitch unless specified otherwise, following the charts on pages
66–68. Trim the gable ends of the side walls close
to the embroidery, leaving complete bars beside
the stitches. Stitch the bay window pieces following the charts on page 69. Also stitch the
sections for the mailbox.

ROOF

Cover each main section with brick stitch over
four bars, using one strand each of black,
brown, and gray yarn in the needle. Work satin
stitch to cover the six narrow edge sections,

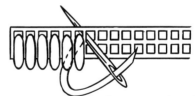

FIG. 41 Roof, *stitching over the edge*

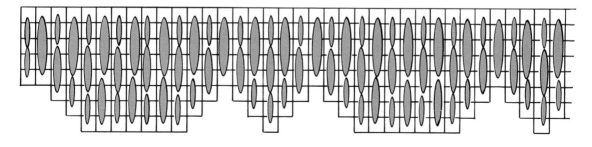

FIG. 42 *The coping*

taking the stitches over one edge (Fig. 41), leaving the other edge uncovered for joining later. Embroider the ridge coping sections as shown in Fig. 42. Cut away the uncovered canvas, taking care to leave one bar beside the embroidery. Overcast the two short and the shaped edges in gray yarn. Embroider the two gable ends and overcast all around with gray yarn. Embroider the eaves in black yarn, using satin stitch on the wide sections, tent stitch on the narrow.

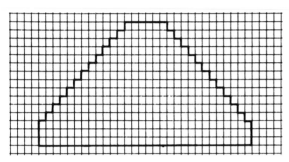

FIG. 43 Gable ends

TO MAKE THE COTTAGE

Use two strands of dark gray yarn for stitching the roof together; elsewhere match the color of the pieces being joined.

For the bay window, cut between the side windows and the central double window of the bay window section, trim off the spikes, and overcast together again in cream. Trim the bay roof and base, leaving one complete bar of plastic canvas beside the stitching, and overcast to the window. Stitch the supports to each lower corner. Place in position on the door side of the house and stitch in place with black yarn along the base and top, cream yarn along the sides. Catch the supports in place at their lower end.

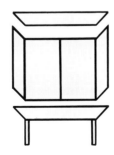

FIG. 44 Construction of bay window

For the mailbox, join the front to the sides and stitch the base in place. Join the roof sections together along one short edge. Overcast the narrow fascia pieces to the long edges of the roof, overcasting the two short edges of the the roof as you do so. Catch stitch the roof section to the box, keeping the back edges in line with the side walls. Overcast the mailbox in position on the front wall of the house.

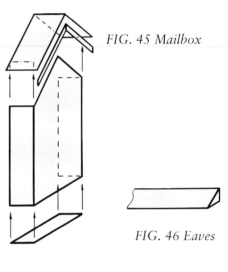

FIG. 45 Mailbox

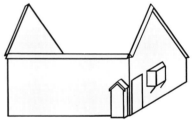

FIG. 46 Eaves

FIG. 47 Walls to base

For the cottage, stitch the eaves together in sets of three, one wide and two narrow pieces along the long edges to form triangular sections, overcasting the short ends as you go.

Overcast the four walls to the base. Join the four corners. Overcast all around the upper edge. Use three strands if this will pass through the canvas.

Using a single strand of black yarn, stitch the eaves in position along the top of each wall, with edges matched up and wide sloping faces uppermost.

For the roof, overcast the narrow edge strips to the roof along the side and lower edges. Overcast the shaped edges of the two roof coping sections (107 x 8), using two strands of the dark gray yarn, and baste to the edge of each roof section.

Overcast the roof edge with the shaped coping sections to the roof ridge (107 x 6), treating the two layers of the roof as one piece.

Catch stitch the shaped edges of the roof coping to the roof. Stitch the gable ends to the front roof and ridge end, using a single strand of dark gray yarn.

FIG. 48 Roof fascia   FIG. 49 Coping sections

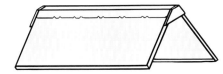

FIG. 50 Roof

LINING THE COTTAGE

This process is very similar to that used in box making and is not nearly as difficult as it might seem. Start when you are fresh, rather than at the end of a long hard day. Clear the table or worktop, reserving one section for a cutting board, one for gluing only, and one for leaving the glued sections while they are setting.

Synthetic velvet jersey fabric is easy to handle and stretch over the cardboard, does not crush or have a nap, and is not too bulky. Some synthetics do not take glue well, so allow them to set before proceeding to the next step.

From the lightweight cardboard, cut one piece 10½ x 7¾in (265 x 197mm).

From the medium-weight cardboard, cut one back wall 9½ x 2in (241 x 50mm), one front wall 9½ x 4¼in (241 x 50mm), two side walls 7⅞ x 7in (200 x 178mm), one floor 9½ x 7½in (241 x 190mm), one front roof 9¹¹⁄₁₆ x 4⅝in (246 x 117mm), and one back roof 9½ x 7in (241 x 178mm).

Try the pieces in position. The side walls go in first, and the front and back fit between them.

Mark the shaping needed on the side walls with a pencil. The top edges should be level with the embroidery on the back wall and the long sloping edges. They should be ³⁄₁₆in (4mm) lower than the ridge and short sloping side walls and the front wall. This allows the front roof lining to rest on the wall lining and be even with the embroidery. The lining should fit snugly without pushing the walls out. Any necessary adjustments should be made as you go along. Trim the side wall cardboard to the required size and try in the cottage again.

Cover the lighter cardboard for the back roof with the cotton lining fabric and glue in position. Cover the remaining cardboard with velvet, and glue sparingly, taking care to trim the corners to avoid bulk. Test the wall linings in the house once more; if correct, glue the allowances and glue the pieces into position. A layer of felt or batting can be placed between the walls and the lining for a more rounded appearance. Slip the covered floor section in place.

Stitch the front roof lining in place, right side facing in. This should rest on the walls, providing a level surface for the embroidered roof to rest on. Glue the rear roof velvet lining in place. The edge should be ½in (12mm) away from the three outer edges of the fine lining and ¼in (6mm) from the hinge side.

Cover the strip of wood with cotton lining fabric, gluing the edges in place. Position across the ridge and glue at each end. Spread glue evenly on the front roof lining, place the roof in position, and hold until set.

THE INTERIOR

Following the chart, cover the shelf supports with tent stitch, leaving the bars uncovered as shown. Overcast the long edges of the shelves and attach to the shelf supports at each end. Overcast re-

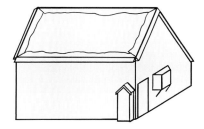

FIG. 51 Front roof lining

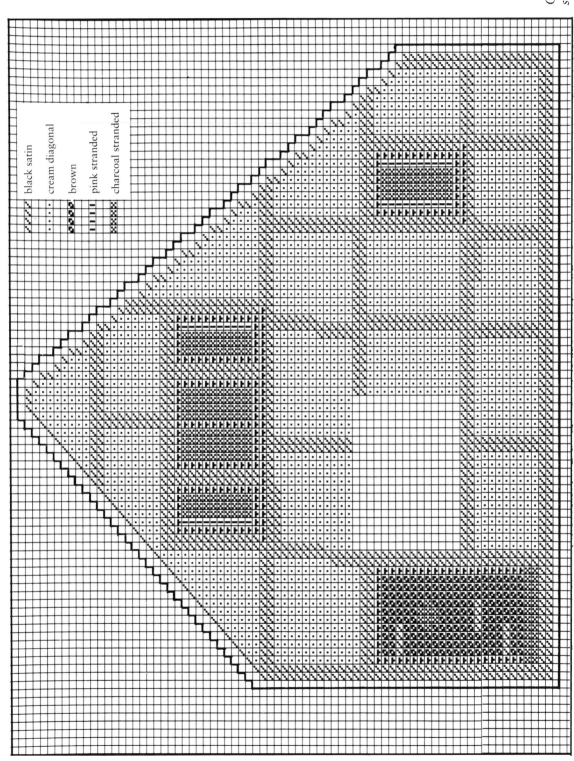

black satin
cream diagonal
brown
pink stranded
charcoal stranded

Cottage right side

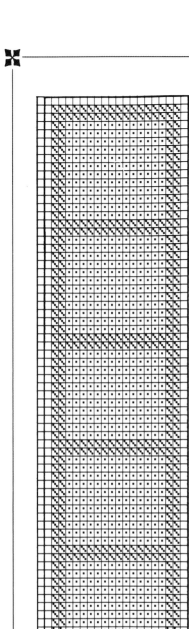

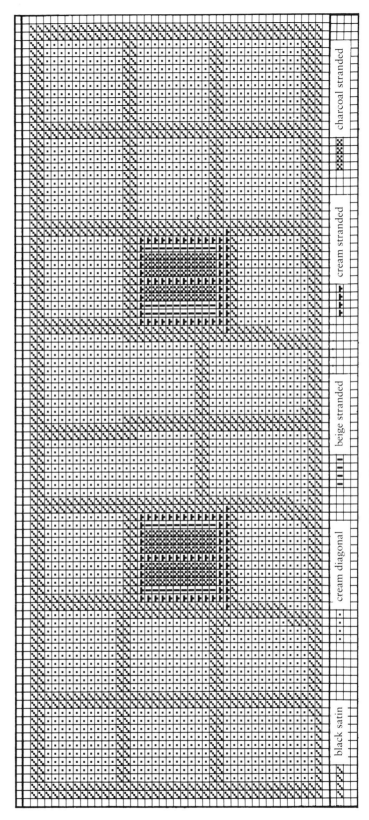

charcoal stranded

cream stranded

beige stranded

cream diagonal

black satin

(above) Back wall; (below) Front wall

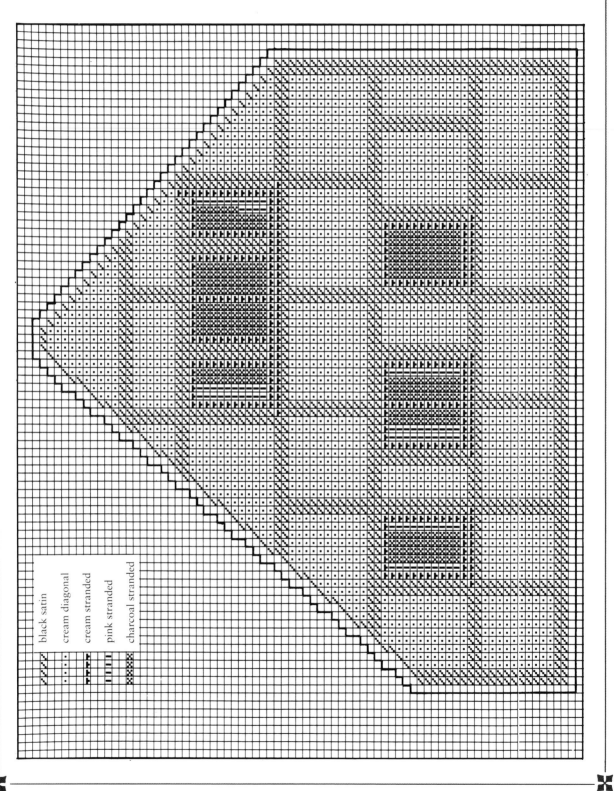

black satin

cream diagonal

cream stranded

pink stranded

charcoal stranded

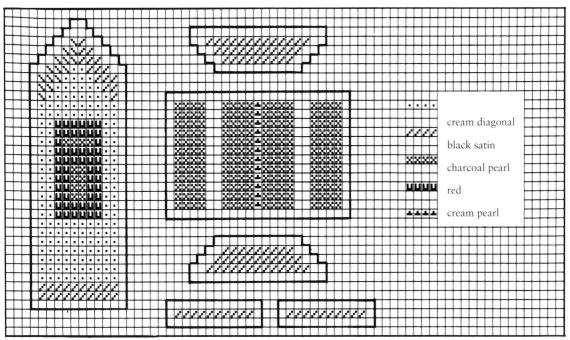

Mailbox and bay window

The legend reads:

· · · ·	cream diagonal
⁄⁄⁄	black satin
✕✕✕✕	charcoal pearl
⊔⊔⊔⊔	red
⊥⊥⊥⊥	cream pearl

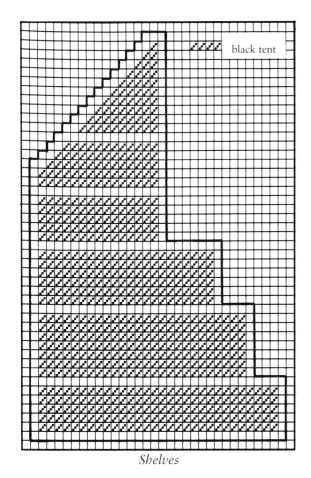

⁄⁄⁄	black tent

Shelves

maining uncovered eges. Cut medium cardboard to fit each shelf, cover with velvet, and glue.

For the pen holder, work a single line of tent stitch in black around the outer edge of the base piece (89 x 20). Next, work a line in red and then another in cream. Fill in the center with lines of satin stitch over two bars in black. Across the plastic canvas for the front (89 x 7), work a line in cream, one in red, another one in cream, and two in black. Cover the two sides (17 x 7) with tent stitch. Overcast the back and the two sides to the base and join the front corners. Overcast all around the edges.

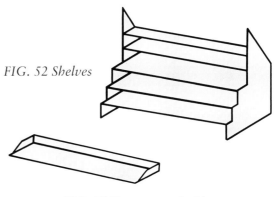

FIG. 52 Shelves

FIG. 53 Tray or pen holder

Address Book and Stamp Holder

To adapt the address book design to fit your own book, simply cut the plastic canvas to fit the covers, making them one bar wider all around than the cover. Cut a spine this length and 5 bars wide. Adapt the embroidery design as required.

MATERIALS FOR BOTH

11 x 14in (280 x 360mm) plastic canvas, 10 bars
   per inch (25mm)
Paterna Stranded Yarn
   four skeins: 263 cream
   three skeins: 220 black
Anchor Pearl Cotton No. 5
   three skeins: 46 red
   one skein each of: 209 green;
   942 yellow

From the plastic canvas, for the address book, cut two covers 64 x 36 bars, two stays 64 x 5 bars, and one spine 64 x 3 bars. For the stamp holder, cut two covers 36 x 29 bars, two pockets 34 x 15 bars, and one spine 36 x 3 bars.

Use the pearl cotton singly for the cross and edge stitch. Use two strands of yarn for the tent stitch.

Embroider the covers in cross stitch following the chart and cover the stays and spine with cream yarn tent stitch. Overcast the long edges of the stays. Baste the stays in position inside the covers, about eight bars in from the outer edge.

Using the red pearl cotton, edge stitch the covers to the spine, then edge stitch all around the outer edge, attaching the stays as you work.

STAMP HOLDER

To avoid bulk, the inside pockets of the holder are two bars narrower than the covers. Omitting the outer line of cross stitch along the top and base, embroider the covers and pockets from the chart and work a line of cross stitch in black down the spine. Overcast one long edge on each pocket section. Overcast to join the covers to the spine. Baste the pockets to the inside of the covers, long edges matched up. Work the outer line of black cross stitch, attaching the pockets as you work. Overcast all around the outer edge.

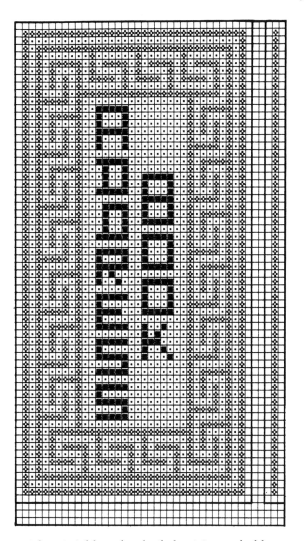

(above) Address book; (below) Stamp holder

▨▨▨▨	red
∙∙∙∙	cream
■■■■	black
◢◢◢◢	green
----	yellow

– 6 –
Dollhouse Dining Room Furniture

*U*NTIL I visited a dollhouse store recently, I had no idea of the fascination of this small world. There, in unbelievable detail, was everything one could possibly need in a real house, from chairs, tables, and sofas down to candlesticks, books, and antiques, all beautifully coordinated and arranged.

A varied selection of furniture and kits is available from specialty suppliers, but by making your own you can be much more imaginative, ensuring the uniqueness of your creation. You can copy items from your own home if you wish.

All the examples in the next three chapters are made to $^1/_{12}$ scale. One foot (300mm) represents one inch (25mm). For example, a bed which usually measures 6ft 3in (1.90m) would measure 6$^1/_4$in (160mm) in $^1/_{12}$ scale.

The main embroidery uses 12 strands of stranded floss throughout. This is rather expensive and is not as easy to use as stranded yarn, but gives a soft, smooth sheen closer to the texture of wood. To prepare the stranded floss, take a length of thread about one yard (1m) long. Thread the needle, then knot the ends together.

Table, dining chairs, and embroidered carpet

Dining Room Furniture

The table top, the back of the side chairs, and the arms of the arm-chairs have a double thickness of plastic canvas for extra stability. The quantities specified will make one table, two armchairs, four side chairs, and the carpet.

Four 14 x 11in (355 x 280mm) sheets of plastic
   canvas, 10 bars per inch (25mm)
9 x 6in (225 x 150mm) cotton canvas, 18 threads
   per inch (25mm)
8 x 6in (200 x 150mm) lightweight cardboard
12 x 6in (300 x 150mm) batting
Anchor Stranded Floss
   44 skeins: 360 brown
   one skein each of: 387 beige; 860 green;
   986 pink; 847 cream
Anchor Pearl Cotton No. 5
   three skeins: 216 green
   one skein each of: 895 pink; 161 blue;
   293 yellow
Paterna Stranded Yarn
   six skeins: 263 cream
Embroidery frame

FIG. 54 Embroidery for chairs

From the plastic canvas, for the table, cut two
pieces 56 x 34 bars, two legs 44 x 22 bars and
two legs 28 x 22 bars, two stay pieces 43 x 4
bars, and two pieces 43 x 3 bars.

For each armchair, cut two backs 36 x 19
bars, four arms 22 x 15 bars, one leg piece 17 x
14 bars, and two seats 17 x 15 bars. For each
side chair, cut two backs 36 x 15 bars, three
legs 15 x 14 bars, and two seats 15 x 15 bars.

For the carpet, cut one piece 113 x 77 bars.

Use twelve strands of stranded floss and pearl
cotton singly. Embroider the furniture pieces in
tent stitch following the charts, noting that some
bars are left uncovered for joining to other sections later. Cut away the surplus plastic canvas,
taking care to leave one bar beside the embroidery. Overcast the inner sections marked with
a cross.

Mount the canvas in a frame and work four
chair seats 1⅜in (35mm) square and two 1⅝in
(40mm) square, using six strands of floss, alternating cream, green, and pink. Embroider the
carpet in cross stitch following the chart. Edge
stitch in green pearl cotton.

TO MAKE THE SIDE CHAIRS

Stitch the lower chair seat to the lower uncovered bar of the inner chair back. Stitch the
back edge of the upper seat to the upper
uncovered bar of the inner back. The other three
edges will be left free for the upholstered seat
to be inserted later.

Place the three leg sections in position and
stitch to the underseat. Join the front corners.

Place the outer back in position, right side
facing out, and overcast to join to the inner back
round the two inner edges, across the top, and
down the sides. Three layers will be joined on
the leg section. Overcast the remaining uncovered eges.

Take the upholstered seat embroidery from
the frame and cut between the pieces, trimming
the spare canvas to ½in (13mm) around each
piece. Cut four squares of cardboard 1⅜in
(35mm) square. Cut three squares of batting

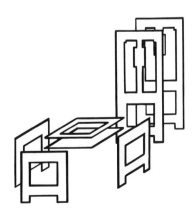

FIG. 55 Dining room chairs

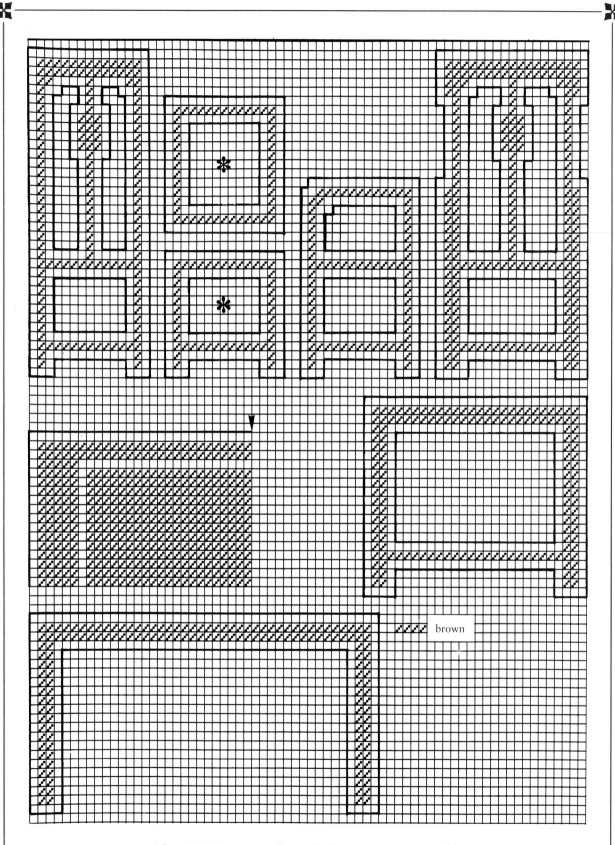

brown

(above) Dining room chairs; (below) Dining room table

for each seat, one the size of the seat opening, one slightly smaller, and one smaller still.

Place the embroidery right side down. Place the batting on top in order of size, largest first, and place cardboard over this. Fold the allowances over and glue lightly in place. Try the embroidery in the chair seat to make sure it fits. Adjust if necessary and re-glue the allowances. Place in the chair seat, padding the seat space if necessary to give a rounded effect. Overcast the three edges to join the upper seat.

TO MAKE THE ARM CHAIRS

Assemble the seats to the inner back as for the side chairs. Attach the underseat to the lower edge of the inner arms and front legs. Join the front and back corners. Join the outer arm section to the outer back and overcast the front edges of the arm sections. Place the inner section inside the outer and overcast together all edges EXCEPT the upper seat and front legs. With only two strands in the needle, overcast the front leg corners to hold the two sections together.

Insert the upholstery as for the side chairs.

TO MAKE THE TABLE

Overcast the long edges of the stay pieces together to form an open-ended box shape, overcasting the ends at the same time.

Place the wrong side of one long leg section against the right side of the undertable, matching the uncovered bars, and overcast to join. Repeat with the other long section and then join the short leg sections the same way.

Overcast the legs together at each corner. Overcast the lower short ends. Using two strands, overcast the stay section to the center of each side leg section. Place the table top over the under section and overcast all around to join.

FIG. 56 Stitching stay to legs

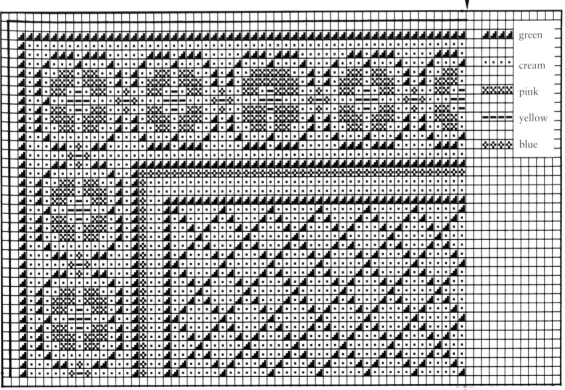

Dining room carpet

- 7 -
Dollhouse
Living Room Furniture

Chairs and Sofa

This classic living room set of sofa and chairs is based on furniture made by Sheraton. The upholstery is embroidered in a stripe design that was very popular in the late eighteenth century. The main sections are made from two layers of plastic canvas for added stability. The upholstery at the back and sides is sandwiched between the layers of plastic canvas, and the seat pad rests on top.

The materials given will make one sofa, two chairs, and the carpet.

MATERIALS

Two 14 x 11in (355 x 280mm) sheets plastic canvas, 10 bars per inch (25mm)
10 x 17in (250 x 430mm) cotton canvas, 18 threads per inch (25mm)
9in (230mm) square of 2oz (50g) batting
10 x 8in (250 x 200mm) lightweight cardboard
Clear glue
Anchor Stranded Floss
    14 skeins: 360 brown
    eight skeins: 387 beige
    four skeins: 20 red
    three skeins: 127 navy
Paterna Stranded Yarn
    two skeins each of: 570 navy; 444 beige; 950 red
one skein each of: 834 orange; 554 blue
Embroidery frame

From the plastic canvas, for the sofa, cut two backs 60 x 29 bars, four arms 24 x 18 bars, two upper arms 20 x 3 bars, two seats 55 x 18 bars, one front 60 x 22 bars, and one front facing 54 x 11 bars.

For each chair, cut two backs 28 x 24 bars, one front 22 x 24 bars, four arms 24 x 18 bars, two seats 19 x 18 bars, four upper arms 20 x 3 bars, and four inside legs 8 x 3 bars.

From the cotton canvas, cut one piece 10 x 7in (250 x 175mm) for the carpet; the remainder is for the upholstery.

From the cardboard, cut 12 pieces 1½ x 1⅛in (37 x 30mm), two pieces 1⅞ x 1¾in (47 x 40mm), one piece 5¼ x 1¾in (132 x 45mm), and one piece 5¾ x 1⅞in (145 x 47mm).

Use twelve strands of floss on the plastic canvas, six for the upholstery. Use a single strand of yarn for the embroidery of the carpet, two for the edge stitch.

Embroider the plastic-canvas furniture sections following the charts, noting that the outer back sections are not cut away above the seat. These should be covered with lines of sloping satin stitch in beige stranded floss.

The front leg section of the sofa is made in double-thickness plastic canvas to strengthen the inner legs. Place the front leg facing behind the front section and work the tent stitch across the front and legs through both layers.

Cut away the surplus plastic canvas, taking care to leave one bar beside the embroidery, and trim off the spikes. Overcast the inner sections, which are marked with a cross.

TO MAKE THE CHAIRS AND SOFA

Make the inner section first by joining the lower seat to the lower edge of the back cross bar. Join the upper seat to the upper edge. Join the inner arm sections to the inner vertical bars. Join the lower seat edges to the lower edge of the side cross bar.

Next join the outer arm sections to the outer vertical bars of the inner chair back.

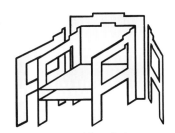

FIG. 57 Assembly of chair or sofa

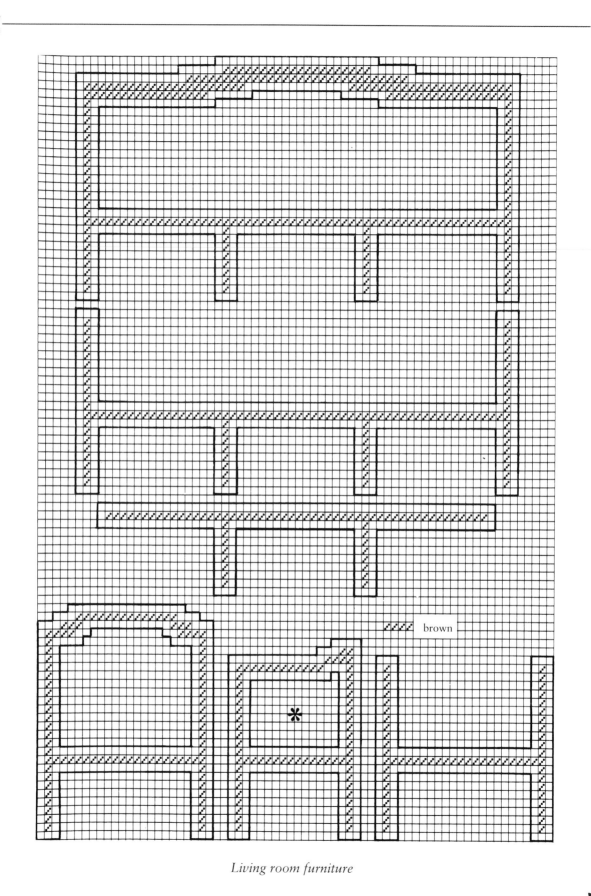

brown

*

Living room furniture

Stitch the front cross bar in place along the upper and lower edges of the seat, and at the sides. Next stitch the four small leg sections in place to complete the legs. Put the upper arm section aside until the upholstery is ready.

THE UPHOLSTERY

Preparing the cotton canvas: It is ESSENTIAL to work on a frame, as the sloping stitches tend to distort the fabric. Since it is very important to keep the stripes running straight, take the following steps to ensure this:

Take care to mount the canvas exactly square in the frame.

Work the satin stitch in the same way as half cross, to give a short sloping stitch on the back rather than a long stitch.

Do not work at too tight a tension.

Mark each section to be embroidered for the furniture with a line of basting stitches or with a disappearing pencil, allowing at least 1in (25mm) between them. Mark the back and side sections just a little larger than the area that will show, as no seam allowances are needed.

For the seat sections, you will need to add allowances because this embroidery will be folded over cardboard to form the cushion. Mark at least ¼in (6mm) extra all around the actual size of the cardboard to allow for this. Following the pattern below, and using stranded floss, work the small sections first, looking out for any sign that the fabric is beginning to distort. If it does, work the dark stripes on the two larger pieces in reverse tent stitch to balance the pull on the fabric. Leave on the frame until required to avoid any relaxation of the canvas.

When ready to proceed, remove the embroidered canvas from the frame. Cut between the sections, leaving very little extra around the small arm and back sections. Leave more allowance for turning over cardboard on the seat sections.

Take the twelve pieces of cardboard for the arms and check them in position. They should fit snugly inside each arm cavity. Trim the embroidery to fit the cardboard along the outer edge of the blue stripes.

Cut three pieces of batting: the first the size of the opening, the second slightly smaller, the third smaller still. Center these over the cardboard in order of size, smallest first. There should be a narrow width of cardboard showing all around for gluing. Spread glue all around this edge, place the embroidery over it, and press in place. Check that the stripes are exactly in line with the edge before allowing to set.

Cover the cardboard for the back of the chairs and sofa in the same way, having first checked that the cardboard is the correct size. It should be a little larger than the opening.

Cover the cardboard for the chair seats with the embroidery. There needs to be very little underlap of the embroidery on the back and side edges, but a good underlap on the front, as this will be visible.

FITTING THE UPHOLSTERY

Slip the embroidery into the arm section, making sure the stripes are vertical. Place the upper arms in position and stitch in place. The rear end of the arm is joined to the back through the bar next to the top edge.

Glue the inner back embroidery in position behind the inner back plastic canvas, taking great care to keep the stripes vertical. Spread glue over the back of this section, place the outer chair back over it, and hold firmly until set. Overcast across the top edge to join. Using two strands of floss, overcast the outer corners to hold them closely together.

Spread glue on the wrong side of the padded seat, close to the edge. Hold in position on the seat until bonded.

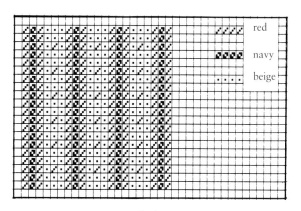

Upholstery

The Carpet

The carpet is taken from an Iranian design from Kusack. It keeps the original lines of the design, but of necessity has been very much simplified.

Mark the center thread of the cotton canvas for the carpet in both directions. This may be done with a fine permanent black felt-tip pen. Place the canvas in a frame and, using stranded yarn, work the embroidery in tent stitch following the chart. The chart shows one quarter of the design. Start with the central medallion, then stitch the main pattern lines before filling in the background.

For clarity, the background is left blank on the chart. The central area is filled in with navy, the next area with red, and the outer with navy.

Remove the embroidery from the frame and stretch as necessary or press lightly under a damp cloth from the wrong side. Trim the seam allowances to about ½in (13mm), and then trim the corners, leaving four threads of canvas. Using the cotton canvas technique (see Chapter 12), work edge stitch all around the carpet.

· · · ·	beige
- - - -	red
XXXXX	navy
T T T T	blue
I I I I I	orange

Living room carpet

– 8 –
Doll House
Bedroom
Furniture

*T*HIS bedroom set is based on a traditional furniture design by Sheraton that is made in satinwood and inlaid with mahogany and other woods. Sheraton's furniture was designed for large houses, and therefore these 1/12 scale models are relatively big. If you are making them for an existing dollhouse, it is important to check the size of the rooms first. The armoire, for example, is 6in (150mm) tall and 5¼in (133mm) wide, but it could be made narrower without losing authenticity.

The furniture has been stitched in light colors to suggest a light wood. The terms *light*, *medium*, and *mahogany* are used for the three shades of stranded floss. Twelve strands of floss are used throughout unless otherwise stated. The main embroidery is worked with six strands of light and six strands of medium in the needle, and is called the main color. This blending gives a slightly mottled appearance of wood to the embroidery. Use two strands of yarn throughout.

The armoire and dresser are made of 10-bar plastic canvas with an inner shell of ultra-stiff 7-bar canvas to give them extra rigidity.

Dresser, armoire, bedside table, bed, rug, and carpet

The Armoire

In the armoire, extra support is provided by the drawer dividers and the inner door frame, which help to keep it in shape. A balsa wood frame glued inside the door frame gives it extra rigidity.

MATERIALS

One 14 x 11in (355 x 280mm) sheet plastic canvas, 10 bars per inch (25mm)
One 12 x 11in (300 x 280mm) sheet ultra-stiff plastic canvas, 7 bars per inch (25mm)
27 x 9in (690 x 230mm) lining fabric
23 x 7in (585 x 175mm) lightweight cardboard
¼ x ¼ x 20in (5 x 5 x 510mm) balsa wood (optional)
6in (150mm) ⅛in (3mm) diameter dowel
⅜in (10mm) Velcro
8 gold buttons or brass paper brads
Clear glue
Anchor Stranded Floss
    ten skeins each of: 372 light oak;
    373 medium oak
    six skeins: 358 mahogany
Paterna Stranded Yarn
    two skeins: 444 beige

From the 10-bar plastic canvas, for the outer armoire, cut two sides 65 x 20 bars, one top 52 x 20 bars, one back 61 x 52 bars, one facing 52 x 5 bars, two doors 35 x 26 bars, one inner door frame 49 x 33 bars.

For the small drawers, cut two fronts 26 x 6 bars, two bases 23 x 18 bars, four sides 23 x 4 bars, and four sides 18 x 4 bars. For the middle drawer, cut one front 52 x 7 bars, one base 48 x 18 bars, two sides 48 x 6 bars, and two sides 18 x 6 bars. For the large drawer, cut one front 52 x 8 bars, one base 48 x 18 bars, two sides 48 x 7 bars, and two sides 18 x 7 bars.

From the 7-bar ultra-stiff plastic canvas, cut one back 40 x 33 bars, two sides 40 x 12 bars, five top and drawer supports 33 x 12 bars, one divider 12 x 4 bars, and six rail supports 5 x 5 bars.

From the cardboard, cut one back 5⅞ x 5in (150 x 128mm); for the inner area, one piece 4¾ x 3⅛in (120 x 80mm), two pieces 3⅛ x 1½in (80 x 38mm), two pieces 4¾ x 1½in (120 x 38mm), and two pieces 3¼ x 2⁵⁄₁₆in (83 x 58mm); for the drawers, cut two pieces 2⅛ x 1½in (54 x 38mm) and two pieces 4½ x 1½in (114 x 38mm).

Following the charts, embroider the doors. Leaving the hinge edge uncovered, work edge stitch around three sides. Work the drawer fronts following the charts. Cover the drawer sides and base with tent stitch using six strands of medium.

Cover the strip for the facing (52 x 5 bars) with lines of tent stitch, alternating mahogany and light. Work similar lines, three stitches deep, across the top edge of the sides (65 x 20). Leave one bar uncovered below this and cover the remaining area with tent stitch in the main color. Cover the top with tent stitch in the main color.

For the door frame, work a rectangle of tent stitch next to the outer edge of the inner door frame (49 x 33), and two lines down the center bars in the main color. Very carefully cut out the two uncovered areas, leaving one bar beside the embroidery. Trim off the spikes and overcast these edges. Center the hooked part of the Velcro on the divider and stitch.

LINING THE ARMOIRE

Using the cardboard shapes as a guide, cut out the fabric for the lining, adding ⅝in (15mm) for seam allowances. Cover each piece of cardboard with fabric. Slip stitch the larger piece to the 10-bar plastic canvas for the armoire back, and set it aside. There should be room at the edges for the needle to pass through when joining the sections.

Attach the door knobs in position. Glue the door lining in place. Stitch the looped part of the Velcro on the edge of the door behind the knobs.

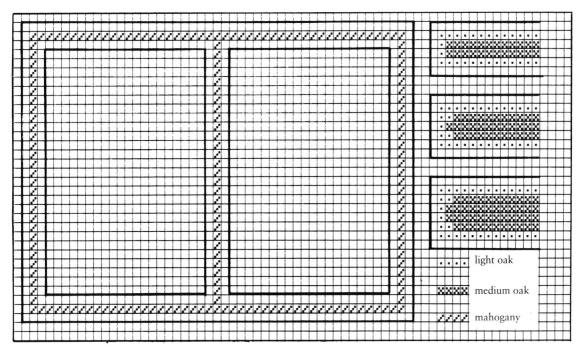

Armoire frame and drawer fronts

`. . . .`	light oak
✖✖✖✖	medium oak
⁄⁄⁄⁄	mahogany

Slip stitch the remaining five pieces of lining to the appropriate plastic canvas to form the interior.

Cut out the center intersection of the six rail supports (5 x 5). Place three together and overcast to hold together. Repeat with the other three pieces. Glue one rail support to each side lining section, about ½in (13mm) from the top.

TO MAKE THE ARMOIRE

For the inner shell, using two strands of beige yarn, join the shelves to the sides, starting with the lowest and stitching the divider to the center of the third and fourth shelves as you do so. Stitch the top and back in place.

Cut the balsa wood into suitably sized pieces to make a frame the size of the embroidered

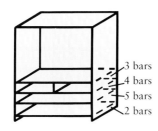

FIG. 58 Inner shelves to shell

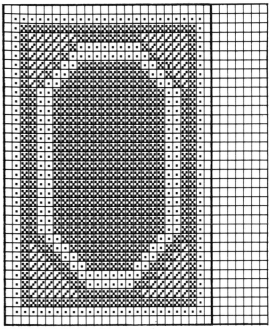

Armoire door

one. Glue together. Slip the balsa wood section inside the frame.

Place the door frame in position and stitch all around. As 10-bar plastic canvas is being joined to 7-bar canvas, it will be necessary to

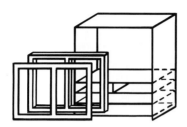

FIG. 59 Door frame

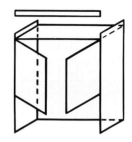

FIG. 60 Assembly of outer wardrobe

work more than one stitch into some holes of the 7-bar canvas. Glue the balsa wood to the back of the frame section. Overcast the remaining uncovered eges.

For the outer shell, overcast the two side sections to the top along the uncovered bars (A). As these stitches form part of the embroidery, be sure to make them look like tent stitch on the right side.

Overcast the top facing in place (B). Stitch the doors in position. Join the back in place and overcast the remaining edges.

Slip the inner shell inside the outer and glue or catch stitch in place.

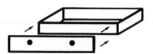

FIG. 61 Drawers

For the drawers, attach the knobs in position on the drawer fronts. Assemble the drawers and overcast the top edges. Check the drawers and fronts in position inside the armoire. The overlap at the center between the small drawers should be less than that on the outer edge. Decide on exact placement and glue the fronts in place to complete the armoire.

The Bed

This bed, complete with mattress and bed linen, is designed as a double bed, but it can be made narrower to suit the size of your dollhouse. The finished size is 4³⁄₄in (120mm) wide and 6¹⁄₂in (165mm) long. If the bed is to fit an existing room, cut the plastic canvas and make a mock-up to check for size.

The mattress is made separately to allow the sheets and bedspread to be tucked in like on a real bed. The materials given are for the bed and bedding.

MATERIALS

13 x 8in (330 x 200mm) plastic canvas, 7 bars per inch (25mm)
13 x 11in (330 x 280mm) plastic canvas, 10 bars per inch (25mm)
16 x 8in (415 x 200mm) evenweave linen, 18 threads per inch (25mm)
9 x 7¹⁄₄in (230 x 185mm) satin
Anchor Stranded Floss

eight skeins: 372 light oak
four skeins: 358 mahogany
one skein: 373 medium oak
Anchor Pearl Cotton No. 5
two skeins: 386 cream
one skein each of: 08 light peach; 10 peach
Paterna Stranded Yarn
three skeins each of: 263 cream, 444 beige

Armoire, bedside table, and rug

From the 7-bar plastic canvas, cut one headboard 34 x 25 bars, one footboard 34 x 17 bars, two sides 44 x 9 bars, and one base 44 x 34 bars.

From the 10-bar plastic canvas, cut one headboard 51 x 37 bars and one footboard 51 x 25 bars; for the mattress, cut a top and base 63 x 49 bars each, two sides 63 x 6 bars, and two ends 49 x 6 bars.

From the evenweave linen, cut one cover 8 x 8½in (200 x 215mm), four pillow pieces 3½ x 2½in (90 x 60mm), and four cushion pieces 2in (50mm) square.

Use the beige yarn for the embroidery on the 7-bar plastic canvas, omitting the bed base. Use two strands of cream yarn for the mattress.

For the bed inner footboard, cover the 7-bar plastic canvas (34 x 17) with lines of satin and tent stitch, leaving the sixth bar from the base uncovered, for the placement of the bed base. Working from the chart, embroider the 10-bar plastic canvas (51 x 25). Starting at the top edge, embroider the headboard (51 x 37) in the same way. Next, work five rows of tent stitch, leave one bar uncovered, and complete with six rows of tent stitch. Cover the outer headboard (34 x 25) with rows of satin and tent stitch.

For the bed sides, work two rows of tent stitch down each short edge and across the top edge. Cut away the uncovered plastic canvas, taking care to leave one bar beside the embroidery. Overcast along the upper edges.

For the mattress, cover the top and four sides with lines of alternating satin and tent stitch. There is no need to embroider the base. Overcast the six pieces into a box shape.

TO MAKE THE BED

Join the inner head and footboards to the bed base along the uncovered bar of plastic canvas. Overcast the lower edge of the bed sides to the base. Place the head and footboards in position on the wrong side of the inner pieces and overcast around the upper and side edges to join them, attaching the legs as you work. Overcast the lower edge of the footboard and legs.

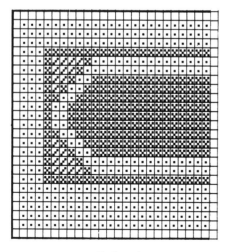

FIG. 62 Construction of bed

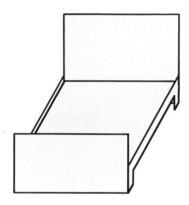

Bed end

THE BEDDING

For the cover, use light peach to work four-sided edge stitch on the linen to yield a rectangle 6 x 4½in (150 x 112mm). Fill in the remaining areas with four-sided and stem stitch.

Work the pillows and cushions in the same way as the cradle quilt in Chapter 1 page 19, omitting the stem stitch if preferred.

For the dust ruffle, fold over a ½in (12mm) seam allowance all around the fabric and baste in place. Secure with a decorative stitch such as stem stitch.

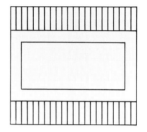

FIG. 63 Bedspread

The Bedside Table

MATERIALS

5 x 8in (125 x 200mm) plastic canvas, 10 bars per inch (25mm)
Anchor Stranded Floss
  two skeins each of: 372 light oak; 373 medium oak
  one skein each of: 358 mahogany; 315 light mahogany

From the plastic canvas, cut a top and under table 26 x 26 bars and four legs 14 x 14 bars.

Embroider the tabletop following the chart. Work four squares of tent stitch next to the edge of the under table. Cover the four legs with tent stitch. Stitch the legs to the under table along the bar next to the tent stitch. Join the corners and overcast around the base. Overcast the tabletop in position.

The Dresser

MATERIALS

6in (150mm) square of ultra-stiff plastic canvas,
   7 bars per inch (25mm)
12 x 10in (300 x 250mm) plastic canvas, 10
   bars per inch (25mm)
Two gold buttons or brass paper brads
$2\frac{7}{8}$ x $1\frac{3}{4}$in (73 x 44mm) mirror
Clear glue
Anchor Stranded Floss
   six skeins each of: 372 light oak; 373 medium
   oak
   one skein: 358 mahogany

From the 7-bar plastic canvas, cut one back 26 x 10 bars, one top 26 x 9 bars, one shelf support 26 x 9 bars, two sides 15 x 9 bars, and one divider 4 x 8 bars.

From the 10-bar plastic canvas, cut one top 41 x 15 bars, two sides 24 x 15 bars, one back 41 x 22 bars, and two mirror pieces 33 x 22 bars. For the drawers, cut two fronts 20 x 6 bars, two bases 17 x 12 bars, four sides 17 x 4 bars, and four 12 x 4 bars.

For the inner shell, take the piece of 7-bar plastic canvas for the back and work four rows of 24 tent stitches wide along the base, leaving the top five bars uncovered for the drawer placement. Work nine rows of tent stitch across the base of the sides.

Take the 10-bar plastic canvas pieces and cover the top and sides with tent stitch. Embroider the back, leaving uncovered the top six bars of the last four bars at each end for the shaped corners.

Work the drawer fronts as in the chart. Attach a knob to the center of each. Cover the drawer sections with tent stitch using six strands of medium. Join the drawer sections into a box shape. Glue the drawer fronts in position.

For the mirror frame front, work a rectangle of tent stitch in mahogany over the bar next to the outer edge. Inside this stitching, work a rectangle in light. Carefully cut out the inner uncovered area, leaving one bar beside the embroidery. Overcast this edge in medium. Cover the mirror back with lines of tent stitch, leaving the sixth bar from the lower edge uncovered.

TO MAKE THE DRESSER

Stitch one edge of the divider (4 x 8) to the center of the shelf. Stitch the shelf to the sides and back,

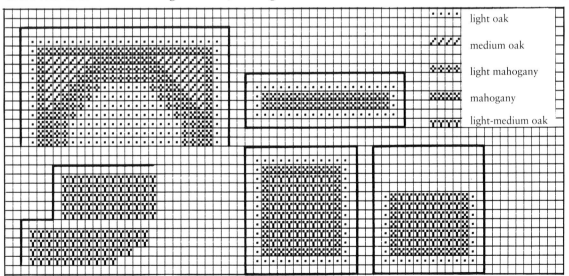

light oak
medium oak
light mahogany
mahogany
light-medium oak

(top left) Bedside table
(below left) Back of dresser
(top right) Dresser drawer
(below right) Stool

Bed, dresser, stool, carpet, and rug

along the bar above the tent stitching, attaching the back of the divider at the same time. Overcast the front edges.

Trim away the uncovered plastic canvas at the top corners of the back section, taking care to leave one bar beside the stitching. Join the table top to the back, taking the stitching through the uncovered bar and overcasting the short vertical edges as you work. Place the sides in position and stitch to the top and back.

Place the mirror back over the back edge,

matching up the uncovered bars, and overcast to join. Place the mirror front in position and overcast around two sides. Insert the mirror glass and complete the stitching. Overcast the remaining uncovered edges.

Spread glue evenly over the back of the inner shell, sides, and back, and along the overcasting at the top edge. Place the inner shell inside the outer section and hold together with clothespins or paper clips until the pieces are fully set.

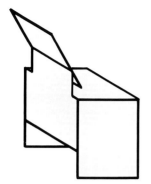

FIG. 64 Dresser

The Stool

MATERIALS

7 x 3in (175 x 75mm) plastic canvas, 10 bars
per inch (25mm)
3½ x 2½in (90 x 63mm) evenweave linen, 18
threads per inch (25mm)
3½ x 2½in (90 x 63mm) contrasting fabric for
lining the seat
2 x 1¼in (50 x 32mm) thin cardboard
Scraps of batting
Clear glue
Anchor Stranded Floss
two skeins each of: 372 light oak; 373 medium
oak
one skein: 358 mahogany
Anchor Pearl Cotton No. 5
one skein: 386 cream

From the plastic canvas, cut four sides 14 x 14
bars, two sides 22 x 5 bars, and two tops 22 x
14 bars.

Use twelve strands of floss throughout.

Embroider the sides following the charts. Cut
out the opening of one seat top and overcast
the inner edge. Join the long sides to the other
top section, then join the inner sides along the
bar above the embroidery, making a shallow
box shape. Place the outer sides in position and
stitch down the sides and across the base, joining the sections.

Work a 2⅜ x 1½in (60 x 37mm) area of four-
sided stitch in the center of the evenweave linen.

Baste the contrasting fabric behind it, using
small stitches.

Place the embroidery over the cardboard, and
glue the allowances to the back, taking care that
the lines of stitching are true with the edges and
stuffing with batting to give a rounded shape.
Place the frame in position and overcast to join
along two sides. Insert the embroidery and complete the stitching, stuffing with batting before
completing.

The Carpet

MATERIALS

One 14 x 11in (355 x 280mm) sheet of plastic
canvas, 10 bars per inch (25mm)
Paterna Stranded Yarn
12 skeins: 756 cream

Using two strands of yarn throughout, work a
border of satin stitch over three bars, then a
rectangle of tent stitch inside the satin stitch.
Repeat the satin stitch and tent stitch borders
once. Work a rectangle of satin stitch over two
bars.

Fill in the central area with Milanese stitch
(see Chapter 12).

The Rug

MATERIALS

One piece 77 x 53 bars of plastic canvas, 14 bars
per inch (25mm)
Anchor Stranded Floss
one skein each of: 860 green; 883 rust; 313
yellow; 160 blue; 275 cream

Use three strands of floss throughout.

This pattern is worked in the same way as
the border of the living room carpet in Chapter
7. The size of the rug can be varied to suit the
room setting.

– 9 –
Miniature Pictures

*T*HESE decoratively stitched pictures are quick to sew and make ideal small projects. The floral pictures are stitched in freestyle embroidery, while the cottage picture is counted-thread embroidery.

The cross stitch cottage picture is worked on Aida fabric with 22 threads to the inch (25mm). Good light is essential for counted-thread embroidery, and a magnifier certainly helps. Working from a chart needs concentration, but the resulting embroidery is attractive. Be warned: It rapidly becomes addictive.

In complete contrast is the freer, more textured type of embroidery used in the four little flower pictures and two miniatures. Here, results can be achieved relatively quickly, without the eye strain of counting the threads. The textured stitches and variation in the thread colors make the pictures particularly interesting.

Pulled-fabric flower pictures and cottage sampler

Pulled-fabric Flower Pictures

These four little pulled-fabric flower pictures have been worked on a synthetic voile-type fabric intended for curtains. Using only straight stitches, French knots, and seeding, they are worked in stranded floss.

Working stitches to a tight tension on loosely woven fabric pulls the fabric into holes. The looser the weave of the fabric, the larger the holes become. Straight stitches worked radially around a central hole give a pretty flower shape. When they are mixed with French knots, a lively variation in texture is achieved.

SPRING IN THE GARDEN

This colorful picture is adapted from a photograph taken from my studio window in spring. The sample was worked by eye, straight from the photograph. The areas of green were reduced, and the two clumps of primula in the foreground enlarged slightly to give more color. The bergenia is really a mauve-pink color that is difficult to match, so I have mixed mauve and pink threads to achieve the right tone for the French knots.

MATERIALS

6in (150mm) square of synthetic voile
5¼in (135mm) square picture frame
4in (100mm) diameter circle lightweight
   cardboard
Greeting card with a 3in (75mm) diameter
   opening
7in (178mm) square of crepe in a dark color
Mat board to fit picture frame, with a 3½in
   (90mm) diameter opening cut from center
15 x 13in (380 x 75mm) batting
Crochet cotton for lacing
Disappearing pencil
Clear glue
Anchor Stranded Floss
   one skein each or small amounts of: 41 salmon;
   75 pink; 118 iris; 108 mauve; 302 yellow;
   268 deep grass green; 876 green; 817 bright
   grass green; 259 light grass green; 376 beige;
   359 brown; 856 olive brown
4in (100mm) embroidery hoop

NOTE: A circular picture frame would be equally suitable, as shown in the alternative version of *Spring in the Woods*, in which case the mat is not needed.

The embroidery may be worked by eye, straight onto the fabric, adapting the areas of stitching as you go, for the desired effect. If you find a guide is really necessary, the outline may be transferred to the fabric as follows:

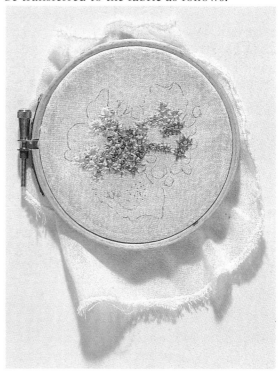

FIG. 65 *Pulled-work embroidery in progress*

Make a tracing of the design on tissue or tracing paper. Center the tracing on the fabric and baste in place. Work small running stitches all around the design, using sewing thread. Pull the paper away carefully. The basting should be removed only when it is no longer needed.

Mark the outer area to be embroidered on the selected fabric. Make it slightly larger than the card opening. Mount the fabric, drum tight, in the center of the embroidery hoop, taking care to keep the straight grain running correctly from top to bottom.

Work the design in straight stitch and French knots, and the background in seeding. Remove from the frame and press, if desired, from the wrong side. Use the opening in the card to check that enough embroidery has been worked, adding more stitching if necessary.

MOUNTING THE PICTURE

Cut five circles of batting, one the size of the card opening (3in/75mm), the others in decreasing size. Place the embroidery right side down, the five pieces of batting centering over it, the largest first, the others in decreasing size. Center the circle of cardboard on top. Fold the excess fabric over the cardboard and lace it, using two yards of crochet cotton. Fold the surplus fabric to the back and lace around, securing the edges with long herringbone stitches (see page 119).

Cut away and discard the two outer sections of the greeting card. Place the square of dark fabric right side down, centering the opening of the card over it. Mark the outline with a disappearing pencil. Cut out the center of the fabric, leaving ½in (13mm) for folding back. Clip fabric to the marked line at intervals of about ⅜in (10mm). Spread glue all around the opening, and fold the fabric back to cover the edge. Pull tightly so the fabric is taut over the edge.

To assemble the picture, place embroidery right side up and apply glue around the edge. Position the fabric-covered mat on top and leave until set. Place the mat on top and mount the picture in the frame.

SPRING IN THE WOODS

This picture is based on a photograph taken on a hiking vacation in the United States and is a memento of good times. We were walking in the Blue Ridge Mountains among bare trees and suddenly came upon this tree of blossoms outlined against the sky.

Follow the materials and instructions for *Spring in the Garden*, using these colors:

Anchor Stranded Floss
    one skein each or small amounts of: 153 blue; 300 pale yellow; 253 light green; 843 olive green; 856 olive brown; 905 brown

SUMMER IN WALES

This embroidery is based on a photograph of Bodnant Garden, Clwyd, taken from a calendar. The dramatic colors are set off by the somber colors of the trees, and a shaft of sunlight lights up the middle ground. The sunlit lawn in the foreground creates further contrast.

Follow the materials and instructions for *Spring in the Garden*, using these colors:

Anchor Stranded Floss
    one skein each or small amounts of: 41 salmon; 35 deep salmon; 68 raspberry; 108 mauve; 98 purple; 89 cerise; 160 blue; 300 pale yellow; 926 cream; 381 brown; 216 green; 218 dark green; 265 grass green; 846 olive green; 259 light grass green; 843 light olive green; 01 white

SUMMER IN A VASE

This embroidery is adapted from a painting by Renoir. The flowers appear almost three-dimensional, seeming to come out of the canvas. The chief interest is in the deep contrast between the background and the flowers, with the dark shiny vase forming a foil in texture and color. The colors have a wonderfully soft appearance, merging with one another to give a rich glow.

Follow the materials and instructions for

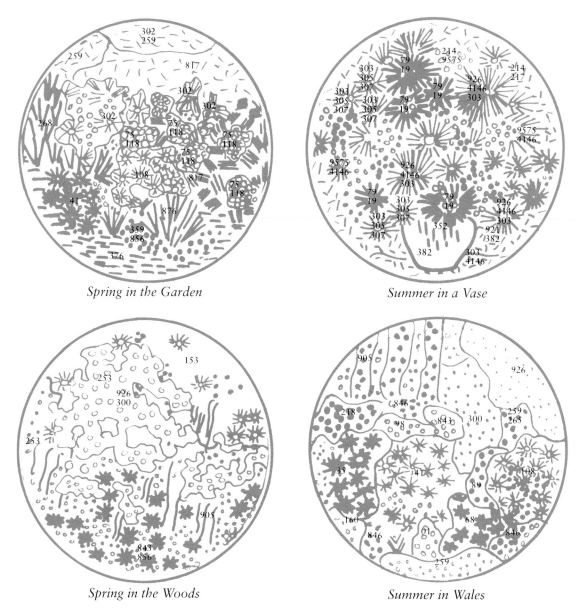

Spring in the Garden

Summer in a Vase

Spring in the Woods

Summer in Wales

FIG. 66 Tracing of four pictures and the placement of colors

Spring in the Garden, using the following colors:

Anchor Stranded Floss
one skein each or small amounts of:
19 pink/red; 4146 pale peach; 79 raspberry;
9575 peach; 352 rust; 303, 305, and 307
yellow; 382 brown; 921 blue/gray; 926 cream;
214 and 217 green

The flowers are all worked in straight stitch, some flowers are pulled into holes at the center, some have centers filled with stitches, and the poppies are worked, leaving a central area for the French knots.

Since seeding is a flat stitch that makes the flowers stand out, it is the stitch used for the background.

Dollhouse Miniatures

Both of these tiny pictures are worked in stranded floss on voile, using the same technique as in the previous pictures. One is the well-known Van Gogh Sunflowers, *the other is based on* Hollyhocks and other Flowers in a Vase *by Jan Van Huijsum. Frames suitable for dollhouse pictures can be purchased from specialty shops. The materials given are enough to make both embroideries.*

MATERIALS

4 x 3½in (100 x 90mm) each of light and black
   lightweight voile
Lightweight cardboard
Inner mat fabric
Batting
Picture frames
Mercerized crochet cotton for lacing
Anchor Stranded Floss
Sunflowers: a small amount each of: 326
   orange; 868 pink/peach; 889 brown; 5975
   red/rust; 366 cream
Hollyhocks: a small amount each of: 868 pink/
   peach; 24 pink; 161 blue; 117 pale blue;
   22 dark red; 46 red; 214 light green; 218 dark
   green; 02 white
4in (100mm) embroidery hoop

Measure the opening of the picture frame and mark this area onto the fabric with a line of basting. Work the embroidery as for the four circular flower pictures.

See Chapter 11 for mounting the pictures. To finish, make a small thread loop near the top of the larger piece of cardboard as a hanger. Place the embroidery in the frame and glue the cardboard on top to hold it in place.

FIG. 67 Thread loop for hanging

Dollhouse miniature pictures and cottage sampler

Cottage Sampler

The technique for this picture is in complete contrast to the pulled work of the other pictures. The formal cross stitches are counted carefully for accuracy.

Miniature pictures make attractive gifts or cards for friends. Stitched to mark a special occasion, such as the birth of a baby, a wedding, or a christening, they give a truly personal touch. A cross stitch sampler of a friend's house would make a very special present.

MATERIALS

6 x 5in (150 x 130mm) white Aida, 22 threads
 per inch (25mm)
6 x 5in (150 x 130mm) black velvet
6 x 5in (150 x 130mm) lightweight black fabric
5 x 3¾in (130 x 95mm) mat board
4¼ x 3⅛in (105 x 75mm) lightweight
 cardboard
Anchor Stranded Floss
 one skein each or small amounts of: 403 black;
 400 charcoal; 883 brown; 216 green; 131 blue;
 33 pink; 305 yellow; 373 beige; 848 light
 blue/green; 47 red
Embroidery frame

Work the main design in cross stitch using two strands of floss. Work the roof in brick stitch using one strand each of black, charcoal, and brown stranded floss in the needle. Outline the mailbox set in black backstitch.

Mount the embroidery over cardboard using herringbone stitch. Cut a piece of mat board to the size required. This should be at least 1in (25mm) bigger than the embroidery to allow a reasonable border to show all around. Cut a piece of lightweight cardboard very slightly smaller.

Cover the larger board with velvet or similar fabric. Cover the smaller cardboard with lightweight fabric, having first stitched on rings for hanging if required. Glue the lined board to the back of the velvet-covered board, covering the raw edges. Spread glue evenly on the back of the embroidery and center it over the velvet-covered board. Make sure that it is centered. Place a weight on top and let it set.

FRAMING

If there is a space between the embroidery and the depth of the frame bevel, cut a piece of backing board that is slightly smaller than the back of the frame, to fill the gap. Place the embroidery in the frame opening and glue the board over it to hold it in place.

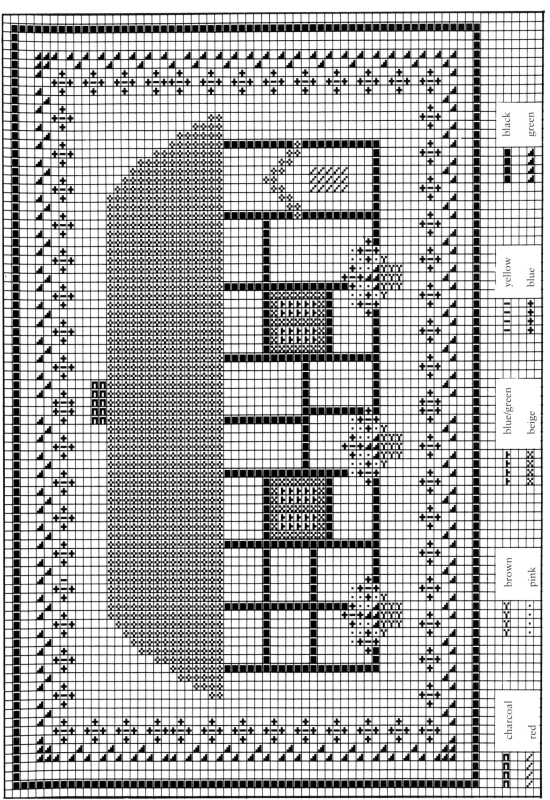

	black		green
■		◢	

	yellow		blue
‖		+	

	blue/green		beige
⊤		⬚	

	brown		pink
Y		·	

	charcoal		red
▯		╱	

Cottage Sampler

– 10 –
Festive Embroidery

C HRISTMAS is traditionally a time for family and friends to gather and bring out favorite decorations. All the decorations given here should last for many years. The ribbon and other yarns will keep their sheen and, since they are washable, will stay looking new for future generations.

Most of the decorations could be adapted in other ways, made on a different-sized plastic canvas, or worked on natural fabrics such as Aida. Cream Aida may become slightly patchy unless washed with care. A cream evenweave linen, which will wash and wear for years, could also be used.

The trees in the border design can be altered in height and width, and the spacing varied. Try to keep an even number of bars between them so that the pointed star can be placed centrally.

*Fruit bowl, candy basket, napkin rings, coasters,
and place mat*

Table Place Mat

A small Christmas plant or a bowl of fruit looks very effective placed on this mat on the table or buffet. The mat could be easily altered in size and shape. To make a long runner, it could be worked with just one central pattern.

Since the sheet size of each manufacturer's plastic canvas varies slightly, it is recommended that you work the outer border of double cross stitch first in order to define the outline of the design. The mesh may then be trimmed as necessary.

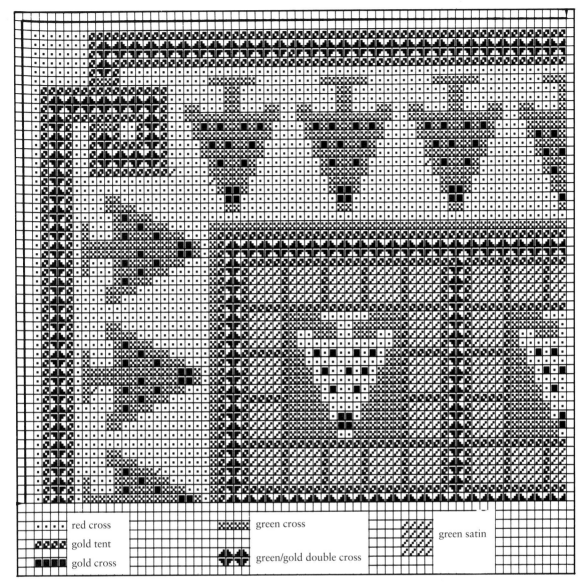

・・・・ red cross	✕✕✕✕ green cross	⫽⫽⫽⫽ green satin
gold tent		
■■■■ gold cross	green/gold double cross	

Christmas place mat: quarter chart

MATERIALS

One sheet of plastic canvas, (for dimensions, see
  below) 10 bars per inch (25mm)
14⅞ x 11¾in (370 x 300mm) cotton or
  cotton blend backing fabric
Anchor Stranded Floss
  fifteen skeins: 46 red
  sixteen skeins: 228 green
One ball of Twilleys Goldfingering

Darice plastic canvas measures 137 x 107 bars,
and for this design it will be necessary to trim
off one bar along the length and width of the
mesh. Uniek plastic canvas measures 141 x 111
bars, and it will be necessary to trim off five
bars in both directions. Use the full six strands
of floss, except for the satin stitch squares, for
which twelve strands will be needed. The gold
thread is used singly. The pointed stars (see page
113) and those on the main tree are worked on
top of the small cross stitch.

Complete the embroidery following the chart.
Trim the mesh as necessary. Edge stitch all
around in red. Fold under and baste the seam
allowances on the backing, then slip stitch in
place using three strands of red.

Coasters

For these you can work four identical coasters, or vary each one slightly as in the examples. Silver yarn, or one of the other colors of goldfingering, could be used as alternatives to gold.

MATERIALS

Four pieces of plastic canvas, 10 bars per inch (25mm), 34 bars square
Four 4⅜in (115mm) squares of cotton or cotton blend backing fabric
Anchor Stranded Floss
    four skeins each of: 46 red; 228 green
One ball of Twilleys Goldfingering

Use the full six strands of stranded floss, except for the satin stitch squares, for which twelve strands will be needed. Use the gold thread singly. The stars on the trees (see page 113) are worked on top of the small cross stitch.

On two of the coasters, work the double cross stitch in red and gold, the satin stitch in green. On the other two, work the double cross stitch in green and gold, the satin stitch in red.

Work the trees in green with a red background, or the trees in red with a green background, to give individuality to each coaster. Edge stitch in the same color as the satin stitch.

Fold under and baste ⅝in (15mm) onto the backing. Slip stitch in place using three strands to match the edge stitch.

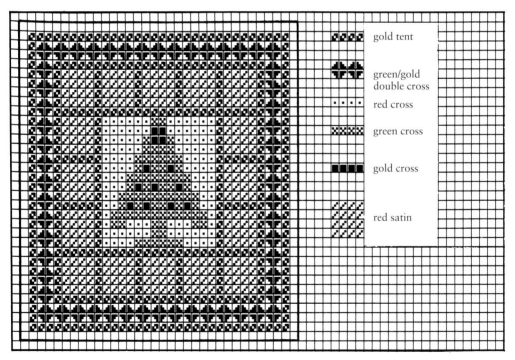

gold tent
green/gold double cross
red cross
green cross
gold cross
red satin

Coasters

Napkin Rings

Both designs complement the pattern of the place mat, and each could be varied slightly to personalize them: Cross stitch could be used instead of satin stitch; alternate squares could be red and green; the Christmas trees could also have individually colored decorations.

The quantities specified are enough to make four napkin rings.

MATERIALS

6in square (150mm) plastic canvas, 10 bars per inch (25mm)

Anchor Stranded Floss
   four skeins each of: 46 red; 228 green

12yd (11m) Twilleys Goldfingering

From the plastic canvas, for the napkin rings with the tree design, cut four pieces 54 x 14 bars. For the square-design rings, cut four pieces 56 x 12 bars.

Use the full six strands of floss, except for the satin stitch, for which twelve strands will be needed. Use the goldfingering thread singly.

For each ring, leave the first and last four or six bars of plastic canvas uncovered and work the chosen design from the chart. Overlap the uncovered ends, matching up the bars, and complete the embroidery by stitching through both layers to join them into a ring. Edge stitch all around in red or green to finish.

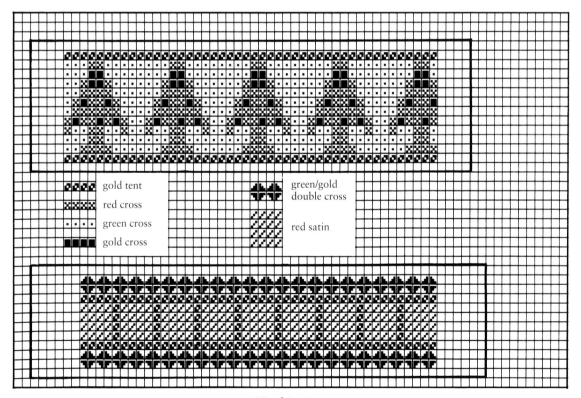

Napkin rings

Fruit Bowl

This bowl is made by slipping an embroidered ring of plastic canvas over an inner bowl lining. The inner bowl is also made of plastic canvas, so it may be removed for separate, more frequent washing.

The embroidered ring could be adapted to make a festive cake band. Measure the circumference of the cake to be covered and make one long strip, allowing an extra couple of inches. Do not join into a ring as it will be overlapped and pinned in place on the cake. The width could be altered by omitting two or more rows of the tent stitch or the double cross stitch.

MATERIALS

11 x 6in (280 x 150mm) plastic canvas, 10 bars per inch (25mm)

18 x 6in (455 x 150mm) ultra-stiff plastic canvas, 7 bars per inch (25mm)

Two 9½in (240mm) diameter plastic-canvas circles

18 x 36in (455 x 900mm) cotton or cotton blend lining fabric

7in (175mm) square of cardboard

12 x 15in (300 x 375mm) 2oz batting

Anchor Stranded Floss
   six skeins each of: 46 red; 228 green

Half a ball of Twilleys Goldfingering

From the 10-bar plastic canvas, cut two sides 29 x 105 bars and two backing strips 8 x 29 bars. From the 7-bar plastic canvas, cut one piece 121 x 18 bars and one piece 22 x 18 bars.

Use six strands of floss for the embroidery and three strands for sewing the lining fabric. Use the gold thread singly.

Baste a backing strip to the right short edges of both side pieces of plastic canvas. Leaving the first four bars uncovered, embroider the sides, following the chart. When the stitching nears the right edge, baste the second length of plastic canvas over the backing strip, matching the bars. Continue the embroidery through both layers to join them. When you reach the right-hand backing strip, overlap the left edge over it and complete the embroidery through both layers, to join it into a ring. Edge stitch each side in gold.

LINING THE BOWL

To prepare the lining fabric, use the length of ultra-stiff canvas as a guide, and cut the fabric for the lining on the bias, with each long side the same length as the 7-bar plastic canvas and

FIG. 68 Backing strip

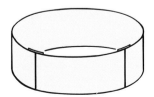

FIG. 69 Overlapped seams

FIG. 70 Fabric on the bias

Fruit bowl and napkin rings

adding ¾in (20mm) to each long side for seam allowances. No allowance is needed on the short edges as the fabric will be stretched tightly over the plastic-canvas lining, giving a smooth fit.

Fold under ½in (13mm) on each short edge and place them together as shown. When the seam is opened out, the straight edges must be in a straight line. Overcast with close stitching, using three strands of floss. Press open.

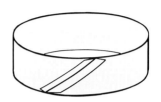

FIG. 74 Seam pressed open

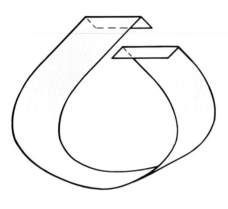

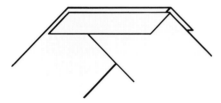

FIGS. 71 and 72 Joining on the bias

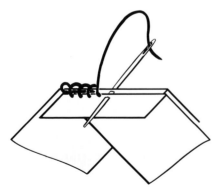

FIG. 73 Completed seam, showing stitches

Join the ultra-stiff canvas into a ring by over-lapping four bars and joining firmly with cross stitch through both layers. Cut a strip of bat-ting to fit inside and baste it, placing the stitches

about 1in (25mm) from the long edges, butting the ends rather than overlapping, to avoid bulk.

Place the lining fabric inside the plastic can-vas, wrong side against the batting. Turn about ¾in (20mm) of lining at the upper edge over the canvas to the outside and stitch in place. Take tiny, almost invisible, stitches on the right side, larger ones on the wrong side. Fold the lining on the lower edge under the batting, so that the fold lies between the two lower bars,

FIG. 75 Lining the interior

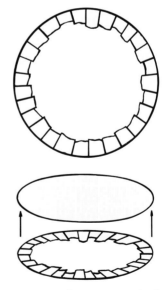

FIGS. 76 and 77 Lining the base

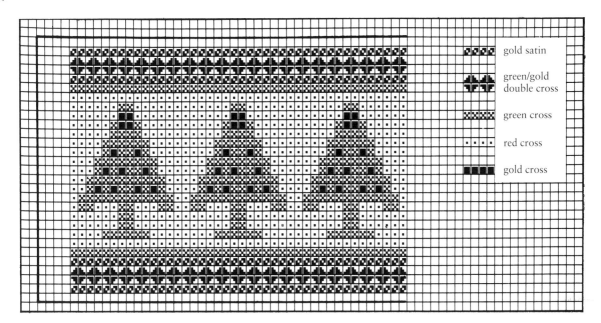

⊡⊡⊡⊡	gold satin
♣♣♣	green/gold double cross
▨▨▨▨	green cross
∙∙∙∙	red cross
▪▪▪▪	gold cross

leaving room for the needle to pass through when joining the side to the base. Slip stitch in place, taking the stitches over every other intersection of the canvas.

For the base of the bowl, cut a circle from the center of one plastic-canvas circle, leaving a frame 10 bars wide. This should yield a circle of 6³⁄₁₆in (160mm) diameter for the base of the lining. The frame may be useful for another project. (As the size of circles may vary according to the manufacturer, check carefully that this measurement will be correct before cutting.)

Cut a circle of cardboard slightly smaller than the plastic-canvas circle. The edge should come

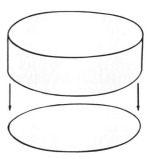

FIG. 78 Side to base

between the outer edge and the first bar. Place the fabric for the base right side down, with the cardboard centered over it. Press the seam allowances over the cardboard to mark the edges. Remove the cardboard and slip stitch the fabric to the plastic-canvas circle to form the underside of the base.

Overcast the prepared lined side to the lined base. Place the embroidery in position over the bowl lining. It should be a tight fit, and no stitching should be necessary to join them.

Cut a circle from the center of the other plastic-canvas circle, one bar smaller than the first. Cover it with batting and fabric. Slip stitch the seam allowance to the wrong side. Slip the circle inside the base to complete the fruit bowl.

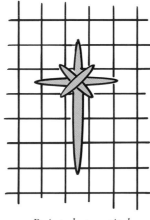

Pointed star stitch

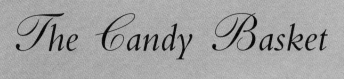

The Candy Basket

This is designed to hold a box of chocolate peppermints. No lining is necessary, as the interior is completely covered by the box. The smaller circle listed below is optional.

<u>MATERIALS</u>

14 x 5in (355 x 125mm) plastic canvas,
   10 bars per inch (25mm)
one 5¾in (145mm) and one 3in (75mm)
   diameter plastic-canvas circles
Anchor Stranded Floss
   seven skeins: 46 red
   four skeins: 228 green
Half a ball of Twilleys Goldfingering

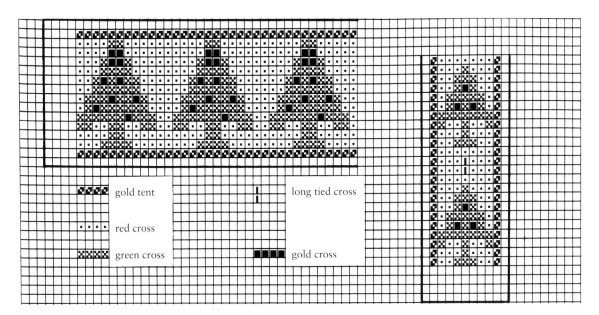

Candy basket side and (right) handle

gold tent

red cross

green cross

long tied cross

gold cross

From the plastic canvas, cut one side 16 x 120 and one 16 x 60 bars, two backing strips 8 x 16 bars, and one handle 134 x 11 bars. The pointed stars (see page 113) and those on the main tree are worked on top of the completed cross stitch. Use the full six strands of floss for the embroidery. Use the gold thread singly.

Leaving the first and last four bars uncovered, embroider the handle. Follow the chart from each end to the middle so the trees all point up. Between the trees, work long, tied cross stitch stars over the red cross stitch background. Edge stitch both sides in gold thread.

Baste a backing strip to the right short edges of the two side sections. Starting with the longer strip and leaving the first four bars uncovered, work the embroidery following the chart. Leave a gap in the stitching at the center of the upper long edge for placing the handle later. This

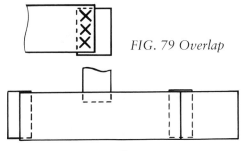

FIG. 79 Overlap

FIG. 80 Handle in position

should be at least four bars deep and extend across the 7th and 8th tree pattern. The exact size does not matter; it just needs to be as wide or a little wider than the handle.

When the stitching nears the right edge, baste the second length of plastic canvas over the backing strip, matching the bars. Embroider through both layers to join them. At the right-hand end, leave fifteen or more bars uncovered.

Baste one end of the handle behind the plastic canvas between the 7th and 8th patterns. Complete the embroidery through both layers.

Overlap the left edge of the side over the backing strip on the right to form a ring, and baste securely in place. Place the free end of the handle beside the backing strip, underlapping it by four bars, and complete the embroidery, securing the seam and the handle.

Embroider the larger circle in satin and tent stitch, alternating the colors, for the base. If making the 3in (75mm) center circle, satin stitch in red and green with a gold Rhodes stitch in the middle. Edge stitch all around.

TO MAKE THE BASKET

Place the side over the base and stitch all around either in edge stitch or overcasting. The former is more decorative, but as 10-bar plastic canvas is being joined to the equivalent of 7-bar canvas, it would be easier to use overcasting.

– 11 –
Equipment and Basic Techniques

PLASTIC CANVAS

Plastic canvas is available with seven and ten bars to the inch, in sheets measuring approximately 11 x 14in (280 x 355mm). The size varies slightly between different manufacturers. Where a full sheet is specified for the projects, this variation has been allowed for. Seven-bar plastic canvas is also available in larger sheets and a variety of stiffnesses. Mesh with fourteen bars to the inch (25mm) is available in sheets measuring 8¼ x 11in (210 x 280mm).

Plastic canvas should be cut with scissors to the size specified, counting bars, not holes. Before cutting out the pieces, plan the position of each piece on the canvas to make sure all the pieces will fit economically. Where edges have been cut, trim off any spikes before starting to stitch; otherwise, the floss or yarn will catch on them.

Plastic-canvas circles ranging from 3in (75mm) to 12in (300mm) in diameter are available. They are either square-mesh circles where the bars lie at right angles to each other (as used in "The Cradle," Chapter 1), or radial circles with the bars radiating from the center. The circles vary in bar count as well as diameter. They can easily be trimmed to a smaller size if required, and the surplus used for picture frames, see Chapter 9.

Basting on plastic canvas should pass between the bars to avoid damage. The outer bar is normally left unstitched for overcasting or joining to other pieces later.

Plastic canvas can be washed with care in lukewarm water.

COTTON CANVAS

The projects in this book use canvas with 10, 12, 14, or 18 threads per inch (25mm). The number of canvas threads per inch (25mm) will dictate the size of stitch and the thickness of thread used to cover the canvas.

For all projects, it is better to work on a frame to avoid distorting the canvas. Allow 1–2in (25–50mm) extra fabric around the design, for attaching to the frame. All stitches on canvas should be worked in two movements. Bring the needle up and pull the floss or yarn through the canvas, take it down, and pull it through.

EVENWEAVE FABRICS

As the name suggests, evenweave fabrics have the same number of warp and weft threads per inch (25mm). Linen has a plain weave, Aida a special square weave. Neither need to be completely covered with stitches. Care should be taken when washing cream Aida as it may become slightly patchy.

Linda is a very finely woven fabric used for counted-thread work, such as the cradle quilt in Chapter 1. Evenweave linen is very durable and can be washed many times and still last for years.

THE CHARTS

Each square of a chart represents one thread or bar of the background fabric.

YARN AND THREAD

Paterna Stranded Yarn is a twisted 3-ply wool yarn. To separate the strands, hold the end of one strand and gently push the other two down against it to remove them. It is available in 8yd skeins or 4oz hanks.

Anchor Stranded Floss is a fine thread with a shiny finish, in six separable strands. Separate the strands as for the yarn.

Anchor Pearl Cotton No. 5 is a twisted thread with a slight sheen. It doesn't have separable threads and is either used singly or doubled.

All care has been taken to record the thread and yarn quantities needed with reasonable accuracy, but amounts used by different embroiderers may need adjustment.

SEWING TIPS

For all thread and yarn, try to keep the tension even when you stitch, giving it a slight pull as you work each stitch so that it lies evenly on the surface. When working on plastic canvas, you may prefer to work at a slightly looser tension than usual, allowing the stitches to puff out for a good cover.

On plastic canvas it is best to work with a maximum 36in (900mm) length of yarn in the needle, except for wide satin stitch, Rhodes, and edge stitch, when about 72in (1.8m) may be used, to avoid joining lengths. On cotton canvas, 18in (0.5m) or even less should be used except for the stitches mentioned. You will need to untwist the threads from time to time.

STARTING AND FINISHING THREADS

Knot the end of the thread and take it through to the back of the work about 1in (25mm) in front of where you are intending to stitch. Work the first few stitches over the thread on the back and then cut off the knot when it is

reached. A new length can be joined in after the first row of stitches by running it through the back of previous stitching. Finish off by running the thread through the back of the last few stitches.

RIBBON

Some of the projects in this book use very fine ⅝in (15m) Offray ribbon for stitching, which gives the embroidery a lovely rich look. For maximum sheen, make sure the ribbon lies flat. As you work each stitch, hold the ribbon between finger and thumb, and guide it through the canvas to keep it flat. Unthread the needle frequently to untwist the ribbon.

NEEDLES

Blunt-ended tapestry needles should be used for working on canvas and for pulled-thread work. They come in a variety of sizes: Size No. 22 is best for working on 14-count Aida. No. 20 is a good general size for working with stranded floss or two strands of yarn. No. 18 is needed for working with three strands of yarn.

MAKING BOXES

BOX WITH SEPARATE LID

Place one side of the box against the base, with wrong side facing and edges matched up, and overcast or edge stitch to join them. Repeat with the other three sides. Stitch the corners. Overcast or edge stitch around the top edge. Make the lid in the same way as the box. If the box is unlined, assemble with the right side of the base uppermost.

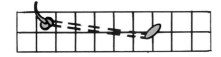

FIG. 81 Starting and finishing

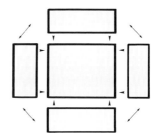

FIG. 82 Box with lid

BOX WITH ATTACHED LID

Make the box as above, but only overcast or edge stitch around three sides of the box and the lid. Place the unstitched edges of box and lid together, wrong sides facing, and edge stitch or overcast to join. Work at a medium tension. Tight stitches will prevent the lid from closing properly.

Make a tassel at the center lid front (see Gold Initial Box, Chapter 4). If the lid does not lie quite flat when the box is complete, dampen a lightweight cloth and place it over the box with a book on top. (This should not be so heavy that it distorts the box.)

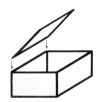

FIG. 83 Box with lid attached

LINING A BOX

Cut the cardboard for lining the box with a craft knife to get a good smooth edge. Use an emery board to smooth the edges if necessary. Ultra-stiff plastic canvas can be substituted for cardboard when lining boxes to make them washable.

Use the cardboard as a guide to cut the lining fabric, allowing ⅝in (15mm) all around for seam allowances. A smaller allowance is suitable for small pieces.

For cutting the batting, use the cardboard as a guide and cut to the same size. If it seems too thick, separate it carefully into two layers.

To cover the cardboard with lining, place the fabric right side down, with the batting, if using, and the cardboard on top. Spread glue evenly around the edge of the cardboard and

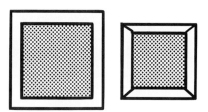

FIG. 84 Covering cardboard with fabric

fold the fabric over, holding it in position until set. Tuck the allowances in away from the edge, so they will not show when the lining is in place.

FIG. 85 Cardboard lining

To insert the lining, glue the longer side linings in place first, followed by the shorter ones, which fit in between, giving the box rigidity. Take great care not to get glue on the right side of the fabric. It may not show up right away, but soon develops into a black mark which is not removable.

MAKING A PINCUSHION PAD

The fabric should be cut in a rectangle which will be folded in half and stitched to make a pad a fraction larger than the finished embroidery. This will give the pincushion a good finish.

Fold under and press the seam allowances on the two shorter edges of the fabric. Fold in half lengthwise and stitch the sides, catching down the seam allowances as you work.

Slip stitch the remaining side, stuffing with yarn or with scraps of batting before closing the gap (see Fig. 86).

BEDDING FOR THE CRADLE

Mattress Make as for the pincushion, stuffing with flat layers of batting and slip stitching the opening invisibly.

FIG. 86 Pincushion or mattress pad

Pillow Fold the fabric for the pillow in half to mark the center. Work stem stitch to form a border on one side, leaving the edges unstitched for the seam allowances. Make as for the mattress.

MOUNTING AND FRAMING AN EMBROIDERY

MOUNTING ON CARDBOARD

Check that all threads ends are neatly finished off, and press the embroidery from the wrong side. Decide how much fabric you wish to show all around the embroidery as a border, and cut the backing board to this size. If the embroidery is to fit in a frame, then the backing cardboard needs to be slightly smaller than the recess.

Cut a piece of batting the size of the frame opening. If you want a circular embroidery to make a dome shape, cut several pieces in decreasing sizes.

Place the embroidery right side down on a work surface, followed by the batting in order of size, and center the backing cardboard on top.

Thread the needle with about two yards of strong thread such as crochet cotton. Fold the surplus fabric to the back on the two long edges, and lace across to secure them with long herringbone stitches. IT IS IMPORTANT TO CHECK ON THE RIGHT SIDE THAT THE FABRIC GRAIN IS LYING ALONG THE EDGE OF THE CARDBOARD. When you reach the right-hand edge, pull the thread as taut as possible and fasten off securely. If the backing is circular, work right around.

Repeat the lacing process in the other direction, tucking in the corners of the fabric.

MOUNTING ON FABRIC-COVERED BOARD

This method is used for the Cottage Sampler, Chapter 9. Mount the embroidery over cardboard using herringbone stitch. Cut a piece of mat board to the size required. This should be at least 1in (25mm) bigger than the embroidery, allowing a reasonable border to show all around. Cut a piece of lightweight cardboard very slightly smaller.

FIG. 88 Mounting the cottage picture

Cover the larger board with velvet or similar fabric. Cover the smaller board with lightweight fabric, having first stitched on rings for hanging if required. Glue the lined board to the back of the velvet-covered board, covering the raw edges. Spread glue evenly on the back of the embroidery and center over the velvet-covered board. Make sure it is centered. Place a weight on top and let it set.

FRAMING

If there is a space between the embroidery and the depth of the frame, cut a piece of cardboard that is slightly smaller than the back of the frame to fill the gap. Place the embroidery in the frame and glue the cardboard over it to hold it in place.

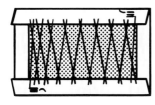

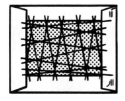

FIG. 87 Lacing with herringbone stitch

– 12 –
The Stitches

COUNTED-THREAD STITCHES

TENT STITCH

Work from right to left with each stitch passing over one intersection of the canvas. This method makes a long sloping stitch on the back and gives a good cover. Subsequent rows may be worked from left to right, but take care that the back looks the same. This stitch tends to distort cotton canvas.

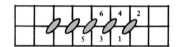

FIG. 89 Tent stitch

HALF CROSS STITCH

This looks like tent stitch on the front, but has a small straight stitch on the back of the work. Start by working from left to right. It does not give as good a cover as tent stitch and is not as durable. However, it takes less yarn and does not distort cotton canvas as tent stitch does.

FIG. 90 Half cross stitch

VELVET STITCH

Begin at the lower edge of the space to be covered. This is a cross stitch with an extra stitch which forms a loop. It should be worked from the base up. The loop may be formed by holding the thread down. A more even result is obtained by wrapping the thread around a knitting needle or pencil. Hold it just below the line of stitching and leave it in place until the row is completed. The loops may be cut or not, as preferred, on completion.

Work the first stitch of the cross from bottom right to top left and then work another stitch ON TOP OF IT, this time making a loop as shown. Complete the cross, thus tying down the loop. Repeat as required.

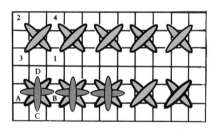

FIG. 91 Velvet stitch

DOUBLE CROSS STITCH

A diagonal cross stitch over two threads is worked first in yarn, and then a straight cross is worked over it. The straight cross stitch may be in the same thread or yarn, or in a contrasting color.

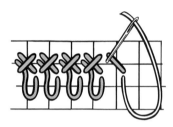

FIG. 92 Double cross stitch

SMALL CROSS STITCH

This stitch passes over one intersection.

FIG. 93 Small cross stitch

LONG CROSS STITCH

A long cross is worked across one thread and up over two, on alternate intersections of the canvas. The stitches of the next row fit in between those of the first for a brickwork effect. Small fill-in stitches are necessary at the edge. It may also be worked diagonally as shown.

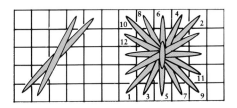

FIG. 96 Rhodes stitch

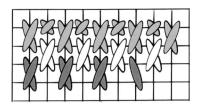

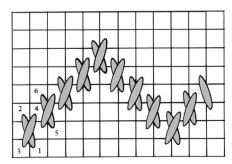

FIG. 94 Long cross stitch

TIED CROSS STITCH

A long cross stitch is worked over three horizontal bars, and a small cross stitch ties it down at the center. Alternatively, it can be worked over two horizontal bars, with a straight stitch tying it down at the center.

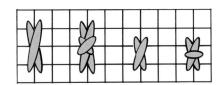

FIG. 95 Tied cross stitch

RHODES STITCH

Long straight stitches are worked rotating around a square. The first stitch is worked from lower left to top right, and after that the needle comes up to the right and goes down to the left of the previous stitch. When the square is filled, a short stitch is made over the center.

SATIN STITCH

Satin stitch can be worked in lines passing over two or more intersections of the canvas. It can also be worked in squares or other shapes.

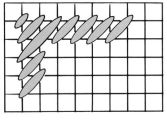

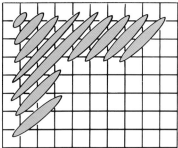

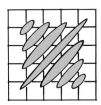

FIG. 97 Satin stitch

BACK STITCH

A stitch is made over one intersection and the needle is brought out at the next hole in front of this stitch. Each stitch is then made by taking the needle back into the same hole and out again two stitch lengths in front.

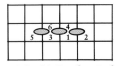

FIG. 98 Back stitch

SMALL DIAGONAL STITCH

A diagonal stitch is worked over one intersection followed by a stitch over two intersections. This sequence is repeated. Subsequent rows fit in the gaps – the short stitch in line with the long, and vice versa.

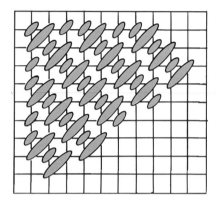

FIG. 99 Small diagonal stitch

BRICK STITCH

This is worked in lines of straight stitches over two or four bars, leaving one bar uncovered between each. Subsequent rows are worked in between for a brickwork effect. The first and last rows need half stitches to fill in the gaps.

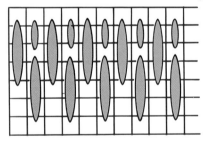

FIG. 100 Brick stitch

MILANESE STITCH

Row 1: Work diagonal stitches over 1, 2, 3, and 4 bars of the canvas. The sequence is then repeated down across the required area.

Row 2: The same sequence is worked to make blocks that fit in between those of the previous row, the stitch over 1 bar being placed in line with the one over 4 bars in the first row. Repeat these two rows to cover the required area,

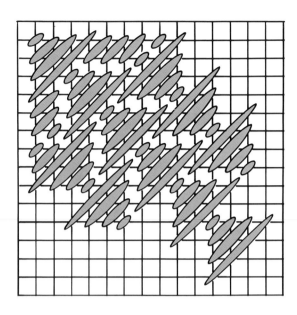

FIG. 101 Milanese stitch

making part stitches where necessary to fill any gaps at the edges.

EDGING STITCHES

OVERCASTING

Simpler to work than the edge stitch given opposite and could be used instead if preferred. You may need double thread or yarn for this stitch.

Always bring the needle up from the back of the work and take it over the edge to make the next stitch. Start by making two stitches in the first hole. Work three stitches into the corners for a good cover.

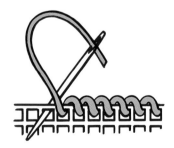

FIG. 102 Overcasting

EDGE STITCH FOR PLASTIC CANVAS

This stitch is used for joining sections together or for covering an edge. It has an interesting

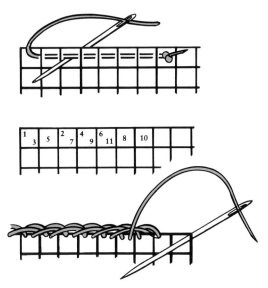

FIG. 103 Edge stitch for plastic canvas

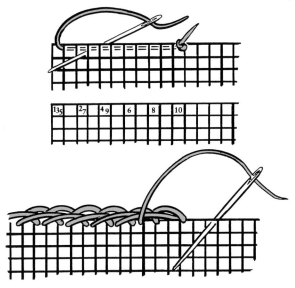

FIG. 104 Edge stitch for cotton canvas

plaited effect, which shows best if worked from the wrong side. Work at a tight tension, except when joining a lid to a box.

Although this stitch may look complicated, it is actually just two movements – forward three bars and back two, repeated. Extra stitches are needed at the beginning and at the end to fill in properly.

1) Bring the needle up in the first hole, take it over the edge, and come out at 2, two bars forward.
2) Take it back over the edge and out two bars back, in the first hole again.

Continue as follows:

3) Take it over the edge, and out three bars forward.
4) Take it over the edge and out two bars back.

Repeat 3 and 4 along the edge until the needle comes up in the last hole. Take it back over the edge and out one bar back, and bring it up in the last hole again. Fasten off securely. At a corner, work three stitches into the corner hole, and continue along the next side.

EDGE STITCH FOR COTTON CANVAS

This is worked in a similar way, going forward six threads and back four, all along the edge.

Fold the allowance to the wrong side between the first and second threads next to the embroidery. One thread should show on the right side, and the holes should match up.

1) Bring the needle up in the first hole, take it over the edge and come out two threads forward.
2) Take it over the edge and out in the first hole again.
3) Take it over the edge and out four threads forward.
4) Take it over the edge and out in the first hole again.

Continue as follows:

5) Take the needle over the edge and out six threads forward.
6) Take it over the edge and out four threads back.

Repeat steps 5 and 6 until the needle comes up in the corner hole. Next, go back four threads and up in the corner hole, back two threads, and up in the corner again. Work three stitches into the corner hole and continue as before.

SURFACE EMBROIDERY STITCHES

STEM STITCH

Worked from left to right. Bring the needle up at the beginning of the line to be covered. Take it down to the right and up again a little to the left, keeping the thread below the needle. Both the lengths and the slant of the stitches can be varied.

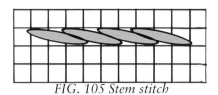

FIG. 105 Stem stitch

RAISED CHAIN BAND

A ladder of stitches is worked first, and then chain stitches, which do not pass through the fabric, are worked over them.

Hold the work in a vertical position and bring the needle up at 1, centrally above the first ladder stitch. With the thread to the right, take the needle over and under the first bar. Now with the thread to the left, work a chain stitch over the same bar. Repeat this process to cover the ladder.

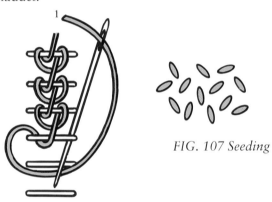

FIG. 106 Raised chain band

FIG. 107 Seeding

SEEDING

Small stitches are worked at random, to give a powdered background.

FRENCH KNOTS

If worked correctly, a pretty rosebud shape is achieved. The secret of success lies in keeping the thread taut against the fabric when pulling it through to the back.

Bring the needle up to the right side and hold the thread in your left hand close to the fabric. Wrap the needle around it once or twice and, keeping the thread taut, insert the point into the fabric close to where it came out. Slide the knot down against the fabric, hold it under your

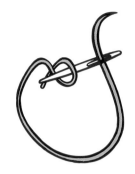

FIG. 108 French knots

thumb, and feed the thread gently through, only taking your thumb away at the last moment.

HERRINGBONE STITCH

As an embroidery stitch, this is worked moving from left to right between parallel lines, taking a small backstitch alternately on each one. It is also used for lacing two seam allowances together when lining a box or mounting embroidery.

FIG. 109 Herringbone stitch

PULLED-WORK STITCHES

These stitches are worked at a tight tension, so that holes form in the fabric, giving an interesting contrast in texture. They may be worked freely on any loose-weave fabric, as in the pin box in Chapter 2 and the pictures in Chapter 9, or on evenweave fabric to give a formal effect, as in the needlecase and pincushion in Chapter 2.

FREELY WORKED EYELETS

Straight stitches are worked into a central hole

FIG. 110 Free eyelets

and pulled so that a hole forms at the center. The looser the fabric weave and the tighter the stitches are pulled, the bigger the hole.

EYELET STITCH

This consists of counted straight stitches worked into a central hole. Worked at a tight tension, they give an interesting variation in texture.

FIG. 111 Eyelet

FOUR-SIDED STITCH

This may be worked over two, three, or four threads. All stitches on the back of the work are diagonal, which means a good pull on the fabric can be achieved. Work from right to left, following the diagram. At the corner, take the needle down to complete the last stitch, turn the work, and bring the needle up in position 3, continuing along the edge as before.

If this is used as a filling stitch, stitch 3-4 will double up with the stitches on the previous row.

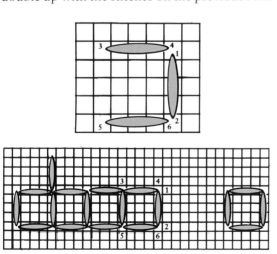

FIG. 112 Four-sided stitch

FOUR-SIDED EDGE STITCH OR PICOT EDGING

At least ¾in (20mm) hem allowance is needed for this stitch. The examples here are worked over four threads. This could be varied to two or three if preferred.

Decide where your finished edge should be. Pull out a thread on this line, and then another, four threads inside it. The stitch is worked in two journeys. A tight tension on the horizontal stitches will give good picots to the finished edge. Work from right to left.

Row 1: Repeat the two stitches across the row, following the diagram. At the corners turn the work and continue as before. Pull out a thread four threads outside the stitching.

Row 2: Fold the fabric along the horizontal stitching along one side and finger-press, lining up the withdrawn threads on front and back. These horizontal stitches will form the picot edge.

Complete the lower edge of the four-sided stitch as shown. Stitches 1 and 2 will go over the edge and out at 3, doubling up with stitch 1 and 2 of row 1.

Before working the last stitch on each side, trim the allowance up to the stitching. Fold the next side's allowance along the horizontal stitching as before, turn, and continue, working double stitches over the corner for strength. Complete the edge this way.

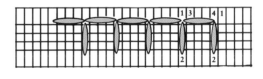

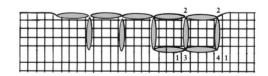

FIG. 113 Four-sided edge stitch

Thread Conversion Chart

Anchor	DMC	Anchor	DMC	Anchor	DMC	Anchor	DMC
19	347	160	813	352	300	846	936
20	816	161	826	358	433	856	3011
41	892	214	368	360	898	859	523
68	3687	216	367	372	738	860	3363
73	3689	218	890	373	3045	876	503
75	3354	259	772	376	842	879	500
76	3731	265	989	381	938	891	676
77	3350	268	3345	382	3371	893	225
89	917	293	727	386	746	895	223
95	554	300	3078	387	ecru	896	3721
98	553	302	743	388	3782	921	931
108	211	303	742	398	415	926	822
118	793	305	725	400	317	4146	754
127	939	307	783	843	3012	9575	758

Acknowledgments

I would like to thank Vivienne Wells for asking me to write this book. I would also like to thank all my friends for their help, encouragement, and infinite patience in helping to work the embroidered samples. These include: Eileen Ellis, Hilary Harrison, Pauline Newland, Wendy Newland, Nancy Perrin, Sheila Tompkins, and all the members of my crafts class, who dropped what they were doing and worked with a will.

Special thanks to Judith Casey for a heroic effort editing my manuscript, and to my husband for taming the word processor, doing the technical drawings, doing the cooking, and tolerating a 5 a.m. alarm for many weeks.

Useful Addresses

UK

Meg Evans
29 New Road
Welwyn
Herts
AL6 0AQ
(Mail order, for most items listed in the projects, including Paterna in 4oz hanks)

Shades at Mace and Nairn
89 Crane Street
Salisbury
Wiltshire
SP1 2PY
(Mail order for a very wide range of supplies, including some beads)

Coats Patons Crafts
PO Box 1
McMullen Road
Darlington
Co Durham
DL1 1YQ

DMC Creative World
Pullman Road
Wigston
Leicestershire
LE8 2DY

The Craft Collection
PO Box 1
Ossett
West Yorkshire
WF5 9SA
(Information on Paterna stockists)

Craft Creations Ltd.
Units 1-7, Harpers Yard
Ruskin Road
Tottenham
London
N17 8QA
(Greeting cards and lining cardboard)

Framecraft Miniatures Ltd.
372-376 Summer Lane
Hockley
Birmingham
B19 3QA
(Picture frames, brooches, and porcelain boxes)

USA

Berroco Inc.
14 Elmdale Road
PO Box 367
Uxbridge
MA 01569–0367
(Information on Twilleys Goldfingering stockists)

Coats & Clark Inc.
30 Patewood Drive
Suite 351
Greenville
SC 29615

DMC Corporation
Port Kearny
Building 10
South Kearny
NJ 07032

Schrocks Crafts
1527 East Amherst Road
Massillon
OH 44646
(Mail order)

Needlecraft Shop
103 North Pearl Street
Big Sandy
TX 75755
(Mail order)

Index

Page numbers in italics denote illustrations.